https://www.stevenlytton.blogspot.com

<u>Mark X</u>

The Killing of Angus Sibbet.

The One Armed Bandit Murder.

<u>By Steven Lytton</u>

<u>ISBN-13: 978-1477586990</u>

<u>ISBN-10: 1477586997</u>

Introduction

Epilogue

Introduction

'Then beneath the bridge, he comes to a giant car, a shroud of snow upon the roof, a mark ten jaguar.' Mark Knopfler (5.15am)

I was still a child in 1971. I remember hearing the adults talking, and sensing their understated excitement, the neighbours over the garden fence talking with my parents; it was a big thing to be happening in the north east. A movie was going to be made, set in Newcastle Upon Tyne starring two of the biggest acting names of the time, Michael Caine and Britt Ekland. 'Get Carter' was the story of a London gangster travelling to the northern city to avenge the death of his brother, based on the book *'Jack's return home'* by Ted Lewis. The man played by Bryan Mosley of Coronation Street fame, portrayed Cliff Brumby who was, so I was told, based on a man called T Dan Smith; a prominent politician who was the leader of Newcastle City Council between 1960 and 1965 and was given the nickname 'Mr. Newcastle' Smith forged business links with architect John Poulson who was one of the advocates of the tower block filled, concrete jungle communities which are now looked back on with horror. This relationship ended in 1974 when he was imprisoned for accepting bribes. John

Osborne played a man called Cyril Kinnear, based loosely on Newcastle's top dog of the day, Vincent Luvaglio, who had changed his name to Vincent Landa. Now, if you read certain newspaper articles and books, or listen to various rumours, you may have been led to believe that his reason for this was because he wanted to use a name that sounded more 'English', this is not the case. I will explain where the name Landa originated from. While living in London, Vincent set up a business with a man named Abbey, which dealt in television and radio provision along with cut price records, Luvaglio and Abbey Enterprises was shortened to 'LandA' Enterprises, this is how Vincent would become known as Vince Landa. He was a Londoner of Italian descent and had moved north to Newcastle from London to set up various businesses' including nightclubs and a coin operated machine business that would provide gaming machines and juke boxes etc. to over ninety percent of the pubs and clubs in the North-East.

'Social Club Services Ltd' was a very lucrative business based in Sunderland, Tyne & Wear. Landa's brother Michael Luvaglio and a well known London criminal called Dennis Stafford, (who was using the alias 'Fielding' at the time) also moved north to join Landa and help with the running of the business. Social Club Services Ltd. also employed a collector by the name of Angus Stuart Sibbet, whom Landa and Luvaglio already knew from their living in London, I will explain how the meeting of the men took place later in this book. Landa spent quite a lot of time out of the country in those days.

Jumping forward about eight years, roughly five miles from where I lived, was a small pit village called South Hetton; I was about fourteen years old at the time. My Father and I were travelling in his 1980 Ford Cortina; we were heading to Durham to visit my Grandparents via Houghton-le Spring, Easington Lane and onto South Hetton. As we passed under a steel built colliery railway bridge, my Father looked at me. "That's Pesspool Bridge, you know, where the body was found in the car". I looked around, there was mainly farmland. As we passed under the steel structure carrying the colliery trains, I looked at him curiously, "So what was that all about then?" He glanced at me, "Remember Get Carter, the film? Well, that was loosely based around things that went on at that time. Back in 67' a guy called Sibbet was found in the back of a Mark X Jaguar, he'd been shot. There were a load of rumours going around at the time, about him stealing money from his boss and a few other theories about why he was done in, but I don't think anybody really knows the real story, well, apart from those who were involved. Vince Landa's brother Michael and another cockney fella called Stafford got sent down for it, mind you, everybody reckons they didn't do it". I didn't say anything at that moment, but as I studied the scene imagining this place as it was on that snowy night, I was fascinated that this kind of thing had happened right here on my own doorstep. "So who's Vince Landa"? I asked. My dad smiled, "Well, he was the big man up here back then before he went off to live in sunnier climates. Every city has a Mr Big, up here in the North East at that time, that man was Landa".

As I got older and left school, by a twist of fate I began working in the gaming industry, and there were a few of my workmates who had been around back in those days of nightclubs, gambling and cabaret. They all had a story to tell; how Landa had put the Kray twins back on a train to London telling them they weren't welcome in Newcastle, how he had thrown other machine provider's machines out onto the streets and demanded that they used his, and many other tales that were probably grossly exaggerated or maybe even completely fabricated. To break the myth, this is the truth about the Kray's visit to Newcastle. When Landa heard that the twins were heading to Newcastle, he informed Superintendant Jack Vinton of the Newcastle police force, and other club owners of the pending visit, he told them what he knew only too well, the dire consequences of the Krays moving in on the gambling and club world of the north east. The twins were followed by the police everywhere they went during their visit to Newcastle before being advised that maybe it would be better if they left, the police handed them a timetable with the train to London underlined. I guess you could say the myths are the breeding ground where legends are born, and how folklore is created. There is though, some truth buried inside the tales that were being passed around, there to be picked out of all the made up stuff that tells a story shrouded in mystery. What has also been forgotten over time is that within this now legendary story, two men were handed down life sentences for the killing of Angus Sibbet. Michael Luvaglio and Dennis Stafford have always proclaimed their innocence and insist that there was a serious miscarriage of justice. Some may say this is fair comment being as there was no forensic evidence whatsoever, and a mountain of withheld evidence and witness statements. I found myself asking, if these men were truly guilty, then why do they still protest their innocence so vigorously, and for so many years after their release? Michael Luvaglio has stated publicly that he does not want to go to his death bed as a convicted killer, because although he has his liberty, he has a lifelong licence attached to his name that labels him 'murderer'. Not only this, but being on life licence means that you cannot vote, you cannot leave the country without government permission and you can be re-called to jail at any time, quite a weight to carry on your shoulders and probably not the definition of 'liberty' that the rest of us take for granted.

What should also be mentioned here is something that most people will not know, Michael Luvaglio was offered his parole earlier, in 1974, on condition that he signed a confession admitting his guilt in the murder, he asked what would happen if he refused to sign and would he still be allowed his release. He was told no, and that he would spend the rest of his life in jail if he insisted on refusing to sign the confession, he told them 'then so be it', he would never sign a confession for something he had not done. It should also be mentioned that when Stafford and Luvaglio were finally released in 1979, that at the time it was unheard of for somebody convicted of murder to be allowed parole without signing a confession.

From what started out as a small project based on my interest in this whole episode of north eastern history, I found myself asking more and more questions, and digging deeper into the facts. My interest gained momentum the more I realised that apart from this all happening so close to where I grew up, a lot of the key locations like the Birdcage Club for instance, would become the places that I would frequent when I started revelling in Newcastle's nightlife, which no matter how many years pass still keeps its party city reputation. Of course the Birdcage Club was renamed the Stage Door by the time I reached drinking age, but the layout had never really changed. I decided to write about my findings and to express my doubts about both the case, and the convictions. As I write this book, the case is now over forty five years old, yet it still holds a place in northern underworld legend and is still talked about over a few drinks in many a local bar, in the now diminishing pit villages of the North-East.

I do not wish to steer readers in any particular direction, I simply want to present you with the facts as I see them and hope you will make up your own mind as to what happened, or more importantly, what *didn't* happen on that winter evening, early morning in 1967. You can see several interviews with Michael Luvaglio if you search through archives, and in every one, you sense an air of sincerity and legitimacy, and that this is a man who has genuinely suffered a major injustice. I will also state here and now, that I never had any communication with anybody directly involved in the case prior to writing this book; the views expressed are based wholly on my research.

It is easy to dismiss the case as something of the distant past, but if you do believe that there was a miscarriage of justice, just stop and think for a moment, let it actually sink in. These are two men who for many years had their liberty taken away from them. Try to contemplate how it must feel to be arrested for a murder that you know nothing about, a murder with no evidence, (not even a murder weapon) and no established motive. Imagine not only the sworn testimony of your friends and neighbours being completely disregarded, but also that of completely independent witnesses with no connection to yourself at all. Of course you would think it ludicrous and would expect to be acquitted and released promptly with an apology for your time being wasted. Well, that is what Michael Luvaglio and Dennis Stafford believed too. This was a case which resulted in two convictions, based wholly on circumstantial evidence that really did not hold enough merit to warrant a trial let alone the life sentences handed out.

This landmark case changed gambling laws in the UK; many of which are still in place, because of the legacy that it left behind. These are the facts regarding the murder of Angus Stuart Sibbet, the case that would come to be known as 'The One Armed Bandit Murder'.

The following list is some of the key people involved in the case:

Angus Sibbet   Victim.

Michael Luvaglio   Charged with murder.

Dennis Stafford   Charged with murder.

Vince Landa   Nightclub owner, businessman
                                  and Michael Luvaglio's Brother.

Tom Leak   Discovered body.

Selena Jones Singer and former partner of Stafford.

Matthew Dean   Doorman of Birdcage Club.

Raymond Dean   Defence Counsel.

 Henry Scott   Prosecution Counsel.

David Napley   Solicitor for Luvaglio.

James Golden   Colliery worker/witness.

Doreen Hall   One of Sibbet's girlfriends.

Joyce Hall   Another of Sibbet's girlfriends
                  (Doreen's sister).

Chapter 1
The Collier's Discovery

The snow had started to fall just after midnight on the 5th January 1967; it had left a light covering on the ground by the early hours of the morning. The shift change at the colliery always happened at 4.30am. Tom Leak, whose only time away from colliery life (which was almost a given for the men of South Hetton in those days) was during his ten year stint in the army. He was a man with a very responsible position at the colliery. He was responsible for handling explosive materials and any lapse of judgement or observation on his part could have resulted in a catastrophe, it is important to remember this aspect of his character as you read this book. After using the pit baths, Leak decided to run ahead of his workmates, Len Ellis, John Leslie Marshall and Billy Jones on the usual ten minute walk to his home. The colliery path led to the A182 road which passed the area known as Front Street in South Hetton. A steel railway bridge which crossed the road carried coal from the colliery; the bridge had no official name but was known to locals as Pesspool Bridge because of it passing over nearby Pesspool Lane.

At 5.15am, as Leak approached the bridge, he noticed a Mark X Jaguar. Instantly this struck him as strange, an upmarket car like that would have been a rare sight in the less affluent, working class mining villages like South Hetton at that time. He got closer to the snow covered car which was parked about fourteen inches from the kerb. He initially thought that the car was parked or abandoned in sheer darkness, but as he neared he saw that the lights were actually on, but were glowing very dimly, the battery had drained. He noted the registration number 'MUP IID' then tried to look through the rear window but the snow covering was too thick. He walked to the near-side and looked through the passenger window. He thought the man slumped across the back seat was asleep, maybe somebody who had drunk a little too much. The head was leaning against the off-side rear window. He then observed a seemingly trivial detail that would later prove to be of crucial importance, the right leg was hanging in the well between the front and rear seats while the left was straight and outstretched across the length of the seat. The car door was not closed properly when Leak opened it. He gripped the man's leg, pulling at it as he spoke with a raised voice, "Hey mate, you can't park here". He touched the skin of the bare leg, as his eyes began to focus he realised by the pallor and stillness of the man, that this was a dead body he had stumbled upon. He would later state that he was no stranger to death and was not overly disturbed by the discovery. He said to himself, "You've had it mate" as he walked away from the car.

He headed back up the A182 to the nearest call box which was about 200 yards away; he passed the three men that he usually walked with. He told them about the body in the car and suggested that somebody go to nearby Welfare Terrace to alert the officer who lived in the local constabulary owned house, while he telephoned the police. Leak reached the call box and dialled 999. He gave his name and address before being connected to the station at Peterlee, approximately four miles away. Leak arrived back at the car at about the same time as the police car and local constable. The two officers who were in the car were James Braidwood Grierson (PC. 1502) and Michael Dominic Hafferty (PC. 1435). They had driven along the A182 already that evening, just before midnight, very close to the prosecution's estimated time of the murder.

Local GP, Dr. John Seymour Hunter's home was less than a mile away from the scene of the murder. He arrived at approximately 5.50am where he carried out a brief examination but had been told by the police not to disturb the body. The police photographer had finished his work taking photographs of the crime scene and the body in the car. It would be 1.15pm, over *seven hours* later before a post mortem took place at the Peterlee mortuary, performed by Pathologist Dr Jack Ennis.

At this stage it is important to note some vital information. Dr Ennis had initially estimated the time of Sibbet's death to be between 12 midnight and 4am; Stafford and Luvaglio had arrived at the

Birdcage club at 12.30 am. But then later, when pressed by the prosecution, Ennis stated that if he had to pin down a time he would estimate 12 midnight. Surely this was self contradicting? If he believed the time of death to be between 12am and 4am then surely that 'pinned down' estimate would have been 2am? When pressed as to why he had stretched backwards the time he had initially estimated, one of the reasons he gave was that he was unaware that Dr Hunter had tested for rigor mortis until that time. Then in another bizarre twist, Dr. Hunter, who had initially stated to Peterlee magistrates that he *had not* checked for rigor mortis on the morning that he was called to the scene of the crime, changed his story too. At the trial he claimed to have lifted the left leg to ascertain the presence of rigor mortis. Now then, if this sudden change of mind were true, and if Tom Leak had lifted the leg, the same leg! (left), that was by his testimony 'straight across the back seat', and the leg was found to be bent when Dr. Hunter and the police photographer arrived, then either rigor mortis would have been broken or was not present. This casts major doubt onto Dr Ennis' estimate as to the time of death, especially when the unheard witness statements contradict it, as does the police officer's statement which claims that he saw the fresh blood oozing from a wound on the body at 5.30am.

The prosecution strangely decided not to call Tom Leak as a witness but decided on using his friend, Les Marshall instead. It was only after Stafford's solicitor's insistence that Leak's testimony which was hugely significant, that it was agreed that he should be called. Why would this be? Surely Leak's statement was one of the most, if not *the* most, vital testimony in the whole case. It could not be ignored simply because it contradicted the statements of others, and was maybe seen by certain parties as, *'inconvenient'*.

Below is the exact transcript from Michael Luvaglio's representation Raymond Dean Q.C. questioning Tom Leak:

Q. Would you look again at photograph number 3, Mr. Leak. You see how the body is shown in that photograph with the knees bent and the left leg uppermost. How were the legs when you saw them?

A. To me, which way I recollect, sir, his left leg was full length on the seat.

Q. Straight along the seat?

A. Straight along the seat.

Q. Not bent?

A. Not bent like that. Not the way I remember it sir.

Q. Did you bend it or did you lift it?

A. No, I didn't bend it.

Q. You just lifted it?

A. I just lifted it.

Leak was oblivious at the time to the chain of events that would follow his discovery of Sibbet's body. He also hadn't realised at the time as he headed to the call box that Sibbet had been shot three times at point blank range.

It is also worth noting at this point that fingerprints and a sample of blood found inside the Mark X Jaguar, did not belong to Sibbet, Luvaglio or Stafford, and that blood found on a phone book in the nearby telephone kiosk matched that of Angus Sibbet. The fact is the dead man could certainly not have left the bloody stain in the call box, which suggests that the killer had left it after being in contact with his victim. It may never be discovered as to the who, and why the callbox was used, but later in this book you will read of a potential witness who tells of how he was contacted that night, and presents a logical explanation to the transfer of blood to the kiosk's telephone book.

The Mark X Jaguar at the scene of the murder

The same spot today taken by the author in 2012

A closer look at the damage to the Mark X,

Chapter 2
Boom Time In The Working Towns

Industry was booming in the North-East. The ship yards, crane builders, coal mines and other heavy industry were on the up, the power of unions had given workers rights and conditions beyond anything that they had known in the past. In a work-hard play-hard environment, the tough, hard working men of the North-East spent the rewards of their labour and long work shifts in the expanding network of high class entertainment, provided by the new style of clubs that were springing up in the towns that surrounded these areas of heavy industry.

Top entertainment was provided by the likes of Tom Jones and Englebert Humperdinck, while top class restaurants, and gaming tables were also provided. A new era in nightlife was born. Angus Sibbet loved to surround himself with the celebrity guests; he counted several of them as personal friends. Sibbet would try to put it across that he was an important figure in the local gambling industry, but in reality although he was a shareholder, he was further down the chain of command at Social Club Services Ltd. That said, he did stand to become a wealthy man in his own right when Landa's accountants suggested going public with Social Club Services. Michael Luvaglio estimates that this would have produced a sum of about eight million pounds, four of which would have gone to Landa, the other four would have been shared equally between himself and Angus Sibbet. Again, to me this suggests that for these men, having found the end of a rainbow so to speak, to have carried out the murder made absolutely no sense. Three intelligent men, all about to become extremely wealthy, throw it all away on that one night in 1967? As a thinking person I find this very doubtful. This was backed up by a businessman based in Teesside who was a personal friend of mine, a man also in the gaming industry and who remains to be to this day, he once said to me, "If things hadn't gone the way they did back then, Landa would probably be a billionaire by now."

Newcastle's clubland had the lion's share of the new style of clubs, included the Dolce Vita, Vince Landa's Piccadilly Club on Bath Street and The Birdcage on Stowell Street. The Dolce Vita club was owned by three brothers by the name of Levy (Marcus, Norman and David), it was they, who played host to the Kray twins, Ronald and Reginald and the down on his luck American boxer, Joe Louis. They were looked after around the town by Paddy Hallet, a north-east hardman who had once been a collector and enforcer for the twins but had moved back north where he ran a company providing bouncers to the pubs and clubs. On that visit the Krays requested to meet up with Michael Luvaglio, he declined before leaving via a rear staircase. It is believed however, that Angus Sibbet did in fact meet the Krays at some point during this visit; however, this was more than likely a minor crossing of paths.

It is probably fair to say that the working class men of those days of heavy industry did not particularly care for the type of people that Stafford and Luvaglio were. They would have seen them as flash because they didn't work in the grinding, manual way that they did. With their expensive suits, flash cars and the way they appeared to have money to burn, resentment would have been strong. This however; should not have in any way influenced the opinions of the public in relation to the crime, who at that time, were being bombarded by the media with stories of British gangland taking a foothold in society. The trials of the Kray and the Richardson gangs in London were headline news. The message being put out by the powers that be was clear, 'make an example of the gangsters'.

Angus Stuart Sibbet had been employed by Social Club Services Ltd since its early days, but again, I must now reveal some facts that will explode yet more myths and incorrect opinions as to how Sibbet came to be involved with Landa. Landa first met Sibbet while still living in London when he undertook some electrical work at the Chinese restaurant which was run by Angus Sibbet and his brother James. Through this meeting

Angus started working for LandA Enterprises (which had now expanded into the providing of pub and club leisure machines like juke boxes, pinball tables etc.) as a shareholder. Michael Luvaglio joined the company in 1958, this is where he also became good friends with Angus Sibbet. During this time, the Kray and Richardson gangs were trying to get full control of the lucrative fruit machine business's that were on the rise due to the newly relaxed gaming laws, threats were being made to operators including Landa via an insurance, or protection if you will, scheme. Landa always refused to pay protection money to the gangsters, which of course made life difficult for him because of the attacks on his business assets. When Sibbet's father took ill, Landa and Sibbet travelled north to Newcastle to pay him a visit. It was during this visit that Landa saw the rich pickings to be made, there seemed to be no pinball tables, juke boxes or fruit machines in the city yet there was an abundance of workingmen's clubs. Three weeks later they had relocated to Newcastle where the business could be made to grow, and was far away from the threats from the London gangs.

Sibbet drove expensive cars and entertained girlfriends in exclusive nightclubs; he even used a chauffeur on occasion. He did all of this on a relatively average wage. How? Simple, he was skimming money from the slot machines. In August 1967, Vince Landa, during an interview with the 'People' newspaper, told a reporter that skimming was almost an accepted practice, in fact one which he claims to have been an innovator of. In those days takings from the slot machines were shared between the provider, i.e. Social Club Services, and the various clubs. It became obvious to Landa that the club stewards had nothing to lose or gain when machines became defective, hence, they could on occasion be out of order for several days unreported. This was not good business; the machines were cash cows and the club owners and machine providers stood to lose a fair sum of money. Collectors like Sibbet, would routinely open the machines, click the counter which registered jackpots using a screwdriver and give the steward five pounds (which was quite a large sum of money in those days) to ensure that the company would be contacted as soon as a machine went out of order, so as they could send out a mechanic to repair them immediately, resulting in the flow of coins being virtually continuous.   Of course the collectors soon realised the potential with this system, if you could clock up one fake jackpot, you could clock up multiple jackpots. Even Sir David Napley when referring to Sibbet, said of his job, that it was 'pregnant with possibilities'. This grew into a thriving sideline for collectors. It has also been suggested that although the machines were emptied on a fortnightly basis, Sibbet would empty them a week early and steal the takings. Again, this is speculation. Landa claimed to have employed a private detective to monitor Sibbet's activities to find out where he was spending such vast sums of money. He supposedly asked the detective, "Well, which is it? Wine, women or song?" The detective allegedly replied, "All of the above". Landa claims Sibbet was skimming somewhere in the region of £1600 per week, however, again, this is merely speculation. Much has been made of this; a lot of people's opinions suggest that this was the motive for the murder. However this doesn't seem rational in my view for the following reasons. Vince Landa, the director of a successful and lucrative company was extremely wealthy, with assets rumoured to be in the region of three million pounds in 1967, which would be worth tens of millions today. Why would a man who was known to have many contacts nationwide, involve his own brother, a staunch catholic with no previous convictions to his name prior to this case, and a friend, who admittedly had a very chequered past, but one which certainly didn't include violence or murder, to carry out the killing? Surely a man of his wealth and calibre would have ensured that he and all of his close associates were miles away from the crime, or at least placed in a position where they would have a cast iron alibi while the deed was carried out. I also doubt strongly that he would have allowed his own car to be used as the transport means for a 'contract killing', and then to have it used as the getaway car, let alone be so instrumental in the whole episode. And, even if he had done all of this, then surely he would have used his contacts to make the car vanish from the face of the earth and would have simply reported it stolen as opposed to having it repaired.

On the 3rd of January 1967, Michael Luvaglio, Dennis Stafford and their girlfriends returned from a holiday in Majorca at Vince Landa's villa. Landa also returned to England with the group, but only to meet an accountant in London and was due to fly straight back to his villa the next day. Michael Luvaglio made arrangements to meet, who he has always maintained to be his good friend, Angus Sibbet, the following day. It is known that the pair met to discuss some business matters, they didn't finalise their discussion so agreed to meet that evening at half past midnight at the Birdcage club in Newcastle, as Sibbet was going to be in the city anyway eating at the Dolce Vita. Sibbet is known to have left the Dolce Vita nightclub between 11.15 and 11.20; this was verified by Photographer, Thomas Oxley, the last person other than the killer, or killers, to see him alive. They bumped into each other on the stairs of the club where Sibbet settled a debt with Oxley for some pictures he had taken.

Landa's E-type Jaguar was being serviced by a garage in the Wheatsheaf area of Sunderland at the time. Michael Luvaglio's own car was also being repaired at the same time so he decided to borrow his brother's car, the E-type, being as Landa was leaving the country and would not need it. Incidentally Angus Sibbet actually drove the two men to Sunderland to pick up the E-Type that day. Stafford had a spare key for the car; they took it after much apprehension from the garage owner, who had been told by Landa not to let anybody else use it. After much persuasion he decided that this order didn't extend to Landa's own brother. Stafford and Luvaglio left Stafford's Peterlee home and headed to Chelsea Grove, Newcastle, to the home of Luvaglio where they were expecting an international call from Landa. The call never came. Then, according to Luvaglio, the pair decided to head into the city centre for their arranged meeting with Sibbet, he never turned up. Luvaglio tried to contact him by telephone and asked Sibbet's mistress Doreen Hall if she knew if he had been delayed, a logical possibility due to the bad weather, but she knew nothing of his whereabouts. Miss Hall would confirm this in court.

At 2am, Stafford left the club to collect some cigarettes from the boot of the E-type. He was questioned as to why he hadn't used the cigarette vending machine in the Birdcage club, to which he explained that he had two hundred duty free cigarettes in the boot of the car which he had brought back from Majorca, so it would have been pointless to buy any in the club. According to Stafford when he reached the car he noticed that there was some damage to the rear end. He brought the damage to the attention of Matthew Dean, the doorman of the Birdcage, who stated that he had heard a sound of a vehicle skidding about twenty minutes earlier. The pair walked to the back of the car where they observed that there were indeed tyre tracks leading to the back of the car which suggested a skid had occurred and had shunted the E-Type forward some yards. This was feasible even if the crash was unintentional, considering the snow that covered the ground. Assuming this was an accurate account of what happened on that night then this was important evidence.

At 2.15am Stafford and Luvaglio claim to have left the club and headed to Luvaglio's Chelsea Grove home to find out whether Landa had called, (he hadn't). They then moved on to Stafford's Peterlee home, where they planned to stay the rest of that night. As the sun rose that morning Stafford reportedly checked the damage to the car in the daylight, after seeing the damage and giving it some thought he decided to have it repaired before Landa returned so as to avoid him finding out. On the way to the garage the pair stopped off at a laundrette to have their holiday clothes cleaned.

Later that afternoon the offices of Social Club Services Ltd were suddenly inundated with calls from the press, which according to testimony is where Luvaglio and Stafford learned of the murder of Sibbet.

Later that day the police received a telephone call, the caller explained that he, or she wished to remain anonymous. It was suggested to them that they might want to go to a garage in the Wheatsheaf area of Sunderland and take a close look at an E-type Jaguar. This strong hint was acted upon straight away by the police. The car was seized and the two men were taken in for questioning. Dennis Stafford and Michael Luvaglio were charged with the murder of Angus Stuart Sibbet. Who made that call? and why? Could it have possibly been the actual killer intent on framing Stafford and Luvaglio? Perhaps somebody with something to gain from the shareholders of social club services being put out of the picture? After all, achieving this would have left an open void in the supply of machines to any interested parties.

Vince Landa, Newcastle's Mr Big in the sixties

Michael Luvaglio (left) & Dennis Stafford

Chapter 3

Smoke To Sticks

In 1934, Dennis Stafford was born Dennis Seigenberg, in the east-end of London near to Petticoat lane. He was the son of a successful bookmaker. He went to school with the Kray twins and as a teenager would have a run-in with the infamous gangsters. It is probably fair to say that Stafford had the most colourful and chequered past in this whole story. As a small child he moved twice, first to Stoke Newington and then to Hackney, where his father bought a house on a new development. He was by all accounts a very good student at his school; teachers would describe him as bright and sociable while fellow students remember him as a very confident boy and a natural leader. They also remember that he was not one to back down in a fight and always stood his ground. At twelve years old Stafford saved a boy from drowning in the Victoria Park Lake by running in, fully clothed and dragging the boy to safety. He was evacuated to Cornwall at the start of the war while his father served in the army, however his father's frequent absence would mean he was lacking a certain level of discipline.

In his teens his courage was tested again, as he left a dance hall in Hackney, London. He saw a young man by the name of Roy Harvey being attacked, he ran to help him fight off the mob that was attacking him. Several men were brought before magistrates but were acquitted. Two of those men were gaining quite a reputation, they were twin brothers. At sixteen, Stafford set up his own slot machine business, after he had been sacked from his job as a waiter after finding it tedious and boring. This was short-lived however, as the man he set up the business with fled with the profits and left him to pick up the pieces; he knew he wouldn't fall for it again, it had been a valuable lesson. Shortly afterwards he was called up to do his national service. He was a private for two years before coming out with only one memento, a Luger pistol. He then helped his father to run the public house that he had recently purchased, the Duke of Wellington, near Spitalfields market, but it wouldn't be long before the lure of fast cars and faster women would divert Stafford's attention. He started to spend a lot of his time in the clubs of the west end of London, mixing with various criminals and finding himself more drawn to the lifestyle that crime could provide.

Stafford's first arrest by his own account was when he got involved in fencing some stolen jewellery that had been obtained during a house burglary. He was having a drink at the Moulton Club in the west end when a police officer entered the club and asked if Stafford owned a car that was parked outside. Even though the car was stolen, he admitted that the car was his. The officer asked him politely to move the vehicle; as he got into the car three plain clothed detectives opened the doors and got in. One of the men told Stafford that they knew the car was stolen and told him to drive to the West End Central police station. On the way the detective who was sitting in the front opened the glove box, he took out Stafford's Luger pistol and looked at him, "Oh dear, you're in serious trouble now, boy". Stafford claims that the gun was merely a souvenir from Germany and that it was always kept in his flat, and that it must have been planted inside the car.

Stafford was stunned when the judge handed down a seven year sentence, he was only twenty two; he decided then and there, he was going to escape. On the 8th of November 1956, he and a fellow inmate called Anthony Hawkes, who was serving a six year sentence for fraud went over the wall after Stafford had made a set of duplicate keys in the prison workshop. During the recreation break he stole two prison guards' coats and a thirty foot ladder, which he casually carried openly across the prison yard. They headed straight to the West End where Stafford had a £200 emergency 'stash'. He was also given a loan of £2600 to help him start up elsewhere by an underworld organisation who have what you might call, a criminal co-operative fund, especially for such occasions.

Stafford and Hawkes headed north to Newcastle, where they used aliases, Paul Lewis

(Stafford) and William Whelby (Hawkes). They took lodgings at a boarding house in Thomas Street, paying the rent in advance. They then rented some upper floor offices in Pink Lane; this street is opposite to the Central Station and was notorious as Newcastle's red light area in days gone by. A sign writer arrived the next day to inscribe the name of the fictitious company onto the door, 'Onalbourne Ltd' Merchants', manufacturers and mail order suppliers of gent's wear. The pair set about acquiring stock on credit and started trading. In a short space of time they had acquired £5000 worth of stock which was stored partly in Newcastle, and partly in London; in warehouses that Stafford had taken over. The company grew and ended up employing several staff. It has been claimed that the superior quality of their goods impressed the wife of a senior police officer so much that she invited Stafford under the moniker Paul Lewis, to dine with the couple; he was even a guest at the policeman's ball. Within three weeks of moving to Newcastle the pair moved into two apartments in Osbourne Road, Jesmond; an upmarket area of Newcastle, the street is now a drinking hotspot for students with many of the hotels that used to line the leafy suburb now being converted into trendy bars and restaurants. The pair became notorious womanisers until one woman, twenty one year old Pat Smithson, who was from Gateshead became Stafford's regular partner. He admitted his true identity to her.

Stafford was always confident that he would always be capable of staying one step ahead of the police, until Hawkes; his business partner took the £200 in cash that the company had accumulated, and vanished. Stafford was furious, he told his employee Gerald Hutton to send him all of the Onalbourne stock, saying that he had a big deal coming off. Unfortunately for him, the police had received a tip-off from an informer; they stormed the Pink Lane offices. Stafford decided to do a vanishing trick; he left Newcastle and headed back to London to make arrangements to disappear abroad. In his usual cocky style he was flaunting himself under the noses of the police, while dining in Winston's club with a blonde cabaret singer; he was spotted by a press photographer who took a picture of him kissing the blonde. Again the police were informed but in the nature of keeping ahead Stafford escaped through a back window. Hawkes was re-arrested in the February. Stafford escaped to Trinidad, now using the name William Birch. He remained on the run for nineteen weeks and four days before being apprehended at the Port of Spain airport in Trinidad after arranging to meet another of his girlfriends there, the police had intercepted a telegram arranging the meet and were waiting for him.

Back in Newcastle, Stafford stood trial for conspiracy to defraud and obtaining goods under false pretences. He was sentenced to a further eighteen months which he was to serve at

Dartmoor prison. Six months later, he would escape again, this time with a fellow convict called Joseph Day. During the escape the pair had jumped into an icy reservoir to avoid the police dogs, Day drowned. Stafford had made every attempt to save his life. After six weeks he was apprehended again, he decided to keep his head down and do his time. He was released in March 1964 but on the 7th of September he was again, sentenced to twelve months imprisonment for theft and then a further six months for possession of a firearm.

Early in 1966, Stafford returned to Newcastle with the singer Selena Jones, in August he took over the managing of the Piccadilly Club which was owned by Vincent Landa. Four weeks after the Kray twins had visited Newcastle, not long after Michael Luvaglio had refused to meet them. The Piccadilly Club burned down after an arson attack on the 25th of September. Landa then offered Stafford the job of booking cabaret acts for various clubs. He was provided with a house at Westmorland Rise, Peterlee. A frequent visitor to the house was Michael Luvaglio with his girlfriend, Pat Burgess; he had also moved north to work with his brother (Landa) at Social Club Services. Luvaglio was also very good friends with Angus Sibbet, who worked as a collector for Social Club Services Ltd. They had known each other since 1959 when they worked for LandA Enterprises in London.

Angus Stuart Sibbet was born in Newcastle on the 2nd of July 1934, he was keen to join the army but was refused on medical grounds having suffered from polio as a child; he appealed so strongly that he impressed the powers that be, and was allowed to join up. After he left the army he settled in London where he ran the previously mentioned Chinese restaurant with his brother James. However, his Father's concern that Sibbet was falling in with the 'wrong crowd' was realised when his son was charged with receiving stolen goods and given a twelve month sentence.

Michael Luvaglio was not so flamboyant as his elder brother Vincent, he was quietly spoken and some say even slightly shy. He had chosen to join the RAF to serve his national service, where he trained as an aircraft loader. After leaving the services, he chose a career in printing. He was living with his parents in Orpington at the time, until he decided to join Landa at Social Club Services. He decided on the move and headed north to Newcastle. His parents soon followed suit and also moved to Newcastle. Luvaglio again, chose to live with them until he moved in with his cousin, Brian Ginger.

Luvaglio soon found his forte, he had a skill for negotiating contracts on behalf of Social Club Services, to overhaul the various clubs with new fixtures and fittings to modernise, and renovate their tired look. His good friend Angus Sibbet was very useful to Luvaglio at this time because of his vast network of contacts. Sibbet had cause to visit nearly every club in the North-East; this created invaluable leads for Luvaglio. These are the twists of fate that brought Stafford, Luvaglio, Sibbet and of course, Vince Landa, 'the bandit king', to the north east of England.

Angus Stuart Sibbet
The murder victim

Chapter 4
Laying Foundations

I will start this chapter by laying out a simple framework, the foundations on which both the defence, and the prosecution, built their respective cases. I will then try to fill in the gaps, of which there are many. It took only nine weeks for the whole trial to be completed. The prosecution's case was something of a house of cards, however, some of those cards seem to be, some may say conveniently, left out of the pack. Even during the trial the case was described as '*a puzzle that could never be solved, as too many of the pieces are missing*'.

The prosecution's case was based on the following opinions:

The police did believe that a meeting was planned between Sibbet, Stafford and Luvaglio at the Birdcage Club. However, they believe that the men met up somewhere between Peterlee and Newcastle, as to why this seventeen mile detour supposedly took place has never been explained. They then claim that the first sighting of the E-type, and the Mark X occurred at Four Lane Ends, where they were in convoy driving slowly out of the South Hetton area on the A182, the time was 11.25pm. They also claim that there was one person in the E-Type and two people in the Mark Ten. Less a mile out of the village, opposite West

Moor Farm, the police claim that the murder took place. They believe that two shots were fired, while Sibbet was still in the driving seat. They also claim that five shots were fired in all, three of which hit Sibbet. They estimate the time of this to be 11.50pm. The nature of the wounds would suggest death to have occurred almost instantly due to the damage of many vital organs.

According to police timing, a cyclist from the colliery called James Golden passed the exact scene of the crime, yet he saw nothing, until two Jaguar cars passed him at speed further on down the road, where they turned right into Pesspool Lane. It is here on this quiet road that the police believe that the men stopped to inspect the damage. It is then claimed that as they drove back towards South Hetton, the Mark Ten stalled because of the damage to the radiator and that they abandoned the car and drove at speed back to Newcastle to establish an alibi. They arrived at the Birdcage Club at 12.30am. Incidentally during my research I drove to South Hetton and emulated a part of the drive the prosecution alleged the men had made that night. I imagined I had a body in the car, and if I were to be stopped by the police, I'd be bang to rights. I stopped opposite West Moor Farm where they claim the murder took place, I then drove the short journey to the turning into Pesspool Lane, I then followed this desolate empty road, the only buildings till you reach Haswell Village are the few farm type houses. Then as you circle back into

South Hetton, you end up back where you started. It struck me straight away that this was a senseless journey to make, it would add to the valuable time that you would crave to escape the scene. If the sound of the gunshots were reported to the police, then by simply blocking the road into and out of Pesspool Lane, you would have painted yourself into a corner. I cannot feasibly imagine that the killers would have been so careless. Bearing in mind that the snow covered country road would have made the driving conditions hazardous and could quite easily have resulted in them becoming stranded.

At 5.15am Tom Leak discovered the body in the car. The pathologist described the body as that of a heavily built man weighing about fourteen stones although no actual weighing of the body took place. He had a thick beard and had been in good health prior to his death. Incidentally PC Cluer, a police officer at the scene stated that he saw fresh blood oozing from the body at 5.30am.This would not happen had the body been dead for nigh on six hours by their estimation. At 9am the car with the body still inside was towed to Peterlee. At 10am the body was removed from the car and transferred to Easington Mortuary where it was 28 degrees f. Dr Ennis commenced his examination at 1.15pm, the temperature was now 64 degrees f. It was ascertained that death was caused by haemorrhaging of the heart and that the fatal shot had entered Sibbet's body at the left shoulder and travelled towards the right hip bone obliterating several vital organs. He would have been dead within one minute of this shot.

At 10.20pm on the 5th of January the police arrived at Stafford's flat. John George Collinson, of the Regional Crime Squad, asked the two men to accompany him to Peterlee police station, to help them with their inquiries into the death of Angus Sibbet. Alarmingly during the lengthy interviews with both men, there was a highly negligible quantity of notes provided by the interviewing officers. Even the Judge found it questionable when the defence solicitors pointed this out, asking that the one sheet of paper's worth of notes to be physically held up for the people in the court to see for themselves. Michael Luvaglio was questioned at 12.20am, Stafford at 1.24am. At 3am the pair were cautioned and informed that they were to be detained in relation to the murder, then at 9.40 on January the 6th the pair were arrested and charged with the murder of Angus Stuart Sibbet.

The defences' case was as follows;

Selena Jones who was Stafford's girlfriend at the time and two other women made statements to the effect that Stafford and Luvaglio, didn't leave the flat at Peterlee until 11.30pm, not 11pm as the police claim. The defendants then drove to Luvaglio's flat in Chelsea Grove, Newcastle, where they were seen just after midnight, before leaving the flat and going to the Birdcage Club, about ten minutes drive from Chelsea Grove. The doorman

Matthew Dean remembered seeing the men arrive at the time they stated. Several witnesses saw the men drinking at the bar, they were tidy and clean, and showed no signs of being agitated or nervous whatsoever. If the police were right in their theory, how could they explain the two men dragging a bleeding body across a snowy and mud covered road to appear immaculate forty five minutes later calmly drinking at a bar?

Stafford only discovered the damage to the car when he left the club to fetch the duty-free cigarettes from the E-Type. Matthew Dean had heard the screeching of tyres twenty minutes prior to this, and also saw the appearance of tyre skid marks leading to the rear of the car.

The judge and jury were never presented with numerous witness statements that contradicted the police theories, which I will show later in the book.

The accused men's movements on the night of the murder at this time become a point of contention. The police claim that Stafford had said during his initial questioning that he had left the flat in Peterlee at 11pm, Stafford flatly denied this as did his solicitor Graham Andrews who had been present during the questioning. This also conflicted with the statements of Michael Luvaglio, Pat Burgess (Luvaglio's partner), Selena Jones and her friend Lilian Bunker. Are we to believe that all of these people at this point were willing to perjure themselves?

When Stafford's counsel, Mr Rudolph Lyons questioned Stafford during the trial the following exchange occurred

Q. About what time was it that Michael arrived with Pat Burgess?

A. Well, as I said initially it was between 10.30pm and 11pm as I was watching a film that was on, sir.

Q. What was the name of the film?

A. What Lola wants.

Q. And what did you do when they arrived?

A. Well, Lilian made some tea and had a snack, well, I don't know, a biscuit or something, afterwards I had a wash and, you know, prior to watching the wrestling.

Q. Did you watch anything else on the television?

A. Well, there was some political thing on, which I turned over to watch the wrestling on ITV. I always watch the wrestling.

Q. Now, what time was it when you left?

A. I thought about 11.30 sir, or after, you know.

Q. Why do you think eleven thirtyish?

A. Well I gauged that we had to be in Newcastle for about midnight, and as I told the police I left myself half an hour to get there.

Q. You went out. Which car did you take?

A. The red and black E-Type, sir.

Q. Why did you go in that car?

A. Well I mean, there is only two of us going there and the Arcadian (Another of Social Club Service's vehicles) is like a big hearse, it was freezing cold and it was a very cold night, and the heater didn't work.

This full account of timing and movement of the accused men was corroborated by five witnesses, three at Peterlee and two at Chelsea Grove where they had gone to await a call from Landa.

Then Lilian Bunker's testimony substantiated the accused men's version of events further, this, bearing in mind, was a young woman who had only known Jones for about ten weeks and under the harsh cross examination that goes hand in hand with a major murder trial. If the prosecution case was right, we are to believe that this woman would be prepared to perjure herself for people she had known for a comparatively short time.

Mr. Taylor for the defence asked her;

Q. Can you say what time they left?

A. About 11.45

Q. Did you actually see them go?

A. Yes.

She was then cross-examined by Mr Scott, she gave the following answers to his questions;

A. They came in at 10.45 and left between 11.30 and 11.45.

Q. They came at 10.30 didn't they?

A. A few minutes before 10.45.

Q. How do you know that?

A. I heard somebody pull up outside.

Q. How do you know what time it was, did you look at the clock?

A. Yes, I naturally wondered who was coming at that time, I looked at the clock.

Q. And it said 10.45?

A. A couple of minutes before.

Q. Were you watching television at the time?

A. Yes.

Q. What was on?

A. I think we had just watched a film or something, then wrestling came on shortly after that.

Q. And you were watching wrestling when they came in?

A. I cannot remember if it was on then or not.

Q. You saw the police and made a statement to them on the Friday, didn't you?

A. Yes, that's right.

Of course it could be argued that with the exception of Miss Bunker, the other two women, Selena Jones and Pat Burgess would have more reason to lie and to give the two men an alibi. Yet, the statements made by all three of the women were made on January 6th, well before they could have known anything of the prosecution's evidence. They couldn't have known whether or not the police had unarguable evidence that may have proved them to be lying hence deeming them guilty of perjury, and, if they were lying as I will explain later, they would have been more likely to claim to have left the house nearer to twelve o clock.

There are two other witnesses who would state that they saw the Red E-Type Jaguar or at the very least an exact model of the same colour, which is very unlikely, outside of Luvaglio's house on Chelsea grove. The first witness was Gladys Hill, she lived next door at number seven, she worked as a manageress at the Excel Bowling Club on Westgate Road, Newcastle. On the 4th of January, she explained to the jury that she and her daughter had left the club around midnight that night as there had been a dance event.

Mr Taylor asked her;

Q. How many minutes walk is it from the bowling club to your house?

A. I would say about five to seven minutes.

Q. And you went directly did you?

A. We came straight home.

Q. So five to seven minutes past midnight, or something like that you arrived home?

A. Yes, it would be.

Q. As you approached your home, did you notice anything about the vehicles in the street?

A. Well, there were cars in the street.

Q. Yes, and outside the immediate vicinity of your house, and the one next door, what cars were there?

A. There were two cars.

Q. Yes, is one of them, well, is one of them there very, very frequently?

A. One is there very frequently.

Q. What sort of car is that?

A. I would say it's a large beigy, bronze colour, er.. I don't know..

Q. Do you know what make or not?

A. No, I don't.

Q. Do you know whose car it is?

A. As far as I know it belongs to the gentleman who is using it now, er, Mr, er, the gentleman who is in the house next to me at the moment.

After a small pause she was then asked about a second car parked outside at the same time.

Q. Can you describe the other car?

A. well it is smaller than the other car.

Q. Yes?

A. It was broad but low and had a black top. A coupe type that you could turn over, soft, that you could turn down.

And the colour?

A. The colour was cherry red I would say.
    She then added, "To me, it would be a sports car".

The second witness to see the E-Type in Chelsea grove that night was Robert Arthur Anderson, a company director who lived at Bishop's Lane, Newcastle. He kept his car in a garage in Mill Lane, the continuation of Chelsea Grove. After watching the end of a television programme that night at 11.50, he drove the car the short distance to the garage. Mr Raymond Dean asked;

Q. To get to the garage in Mill Lane, what route do you take?

A. Well, I pass through Chelsea Grove, Mill Lane is the junction of Chelsea Grove.

Q. That is what I wanted to get at, you pass along Chelsea grove do you?

A. Yes

Q. Do you remember the day when the news was released or announced of this murder having been committed?

A. Yes.

Q. On the previous night before the news was announced did you put your car away?

A. Yes.

Q. Did you go along Chelsea grove?

A. I did, yes.

Q. About what time?

A. Twelve, or thereabouts.

Q. Did you notice any vehicle in Chelsea grove that you recognised?

A. I notice the E-Type Jaguar was outside in Chelsea Grove yes.

Q. You say the E-Type Jaguar, Which E-type?

A. Well, I took it to be Mr Landa's.

Q. You knew he had an E-Type Jaguar did you?

A. Yes.

Q. Did you notice any more about it than that, or not?

A. No, I noticed the lights; it was with the lights and when I passed it I slowed down to see if anybody was in it.

Mr Scott cross-examined. He suggested that the time was maybe a bit later than Mr Anderson had estimated, maybe around 12.30. Mr Anderson was adamant, it was definitely no later than 12.10.

When asked how he could be so sure he replied, "Well, because I was indoors about 12.15 after parking the car. I had been watching the television and could recall the times from that. If Mr Anderson was correct in his timing, then if we are to believe as evidence supports, that Angus Sibbet did not leave the Dolce Vita Club till 11.20pm, then it would be virtually an impossible feat for him to have got to South Hetton by midnight. It is not in question that Sibbet did drive to South Hetton, but why did he? That only allowed just over an hour to get back to his meet with Stafford and Luvaglio, maybe to meet a woman? He was a well known womaniser. Maybe a deal on the side of his dealings with the accused, he was after all something of a wheeler dealer character. Interestingly Sibbet's knees incurred abrasions yet, the knee area of his trousers was scuff-free. Is it possible that his trousers were put on after he was killed? If so, where did this happen?

Are we now to believe that these two witnesses were lying too? Because if they weren't, then as I will explain, the prosecution's case relating to the E-type's movements that night, should have been completely disregarded. Mr Anderson did know Vincent Landa and his brother Michael Luvaglio as he had done some work for their company, Gladys Hill knew Michael Luvaglio in the same way most people know their neighbours, they had chatted on occasion. Would either of these two people, really risk lying for people who were little more than acquaintances?

The cabaret act on the night in was an act called, 'The Allen and James duo'. On the night in question they had cut their act short as guitarist John Michael McGarry had a stomach bug, it was between 12.20 and 12.30. As he was leaving the rear area of the stage he threw back a swing door which knocked a man, the man was Dennis Stafford. McGarry confirmed this with certainty, he knew Stafford from the Piccadilly Club. Here is the transcript from the trial, Mr Taylor addressing McGarry;

Q. Well, did you see who that person was?

A. Yes.

Q. Who was that?

A. It was Dennis Stafford.

Matthew Dean the doorman of the Birdcage estimated that the two men had arrived at the club at approximately 12.30. Then John Bowden who was the manager of the Birdcage Club who although had not seen the two men (Stafford and Luvaglio) enter the club, he does recall seeing them very shortly after the cabaret had finished their act. What is remarkable, given the very short timeframe the prosecution would have the jury believe that the crime had been perpetrated, is that every witness who saw the men concurred that they were neat, clean and not at all showing signs of anxiety. Given the margin of time the men had to travel the seventeen miles to Newcastle, according to the prosecution, it would appear they also had time to clean their clothes and shoes on the way too, which would surely have shown signs of debris had they truly been dragging a body through mud and snow, one that would have been bleeding profusely, and then pushing it into the back of a car.

Mr Lyons questioned the Club's manager John Bowden;

Q. You saw them come in. Did you notice anything strange about them?

A. No sir, no.

Q. What about their cleanliness?

A. Cleanliness sir?

Q. Yes, their clothes and faces, and so on.

A. They were clean.

Then the second witness to this point, Matthew Dean was called to give his version of events.

Q. Did Mr Luvaglio and Mr Stafford seem clean to you?

A. Yes.

Q. And tidy?

A. Yes.

Q. Did you see any mud on them at all, or anything like that?

A. No.

Then, according to Stafford they were waiting in the club for Sibbet to arrive, until an hour or so passed which is when Luvaglio telephoned Doreen Hall's flat and asked her what had happened to him. This was confirmed when she was questioned by Mr Castle-Miller;

Q. Did the telephone ring?

A. Yes.

Q. What time was that?

A. About 1.20am.

Q. Who spoke to you?

A. Michael.

Q. Is that Luvaglio?

A. Yes.

Q. Did you recognise his voice?

A. Yes.

Q. What did he say to you?

A. He asked me if Angus was back, I said no.

Q. Yes, and when you said no, what did he say then, if anything?

A. I said, 'Haven't you seen him this evening'. And he said no.

Q. Did Michael Luvaglio say from where he was ringing?

A. Yes.

Q. Where was that?

A. The Birdcage.

At about 1.45am Stafford and Luvaglio had some coffee and snacks in the Birdcage, they had wanted something more substantial but the kitchens were closed by that time. At 2am, this was when Stafford decided to collect some duty-free cigarettes from the E-Type, and this, is when he discovered the damage to the rear of it. Apart from the broken tail lights the car had been shunted by the impact and was about fifteen feet from where he had parked it. Tyre trails and skid marks also backed this up.

Mr Castle-Miller then questioned Mr Dean who explained;

A. About two seconds later he came back in and said, 'someone has hit the back of my car'. So I went out to have a look.

Q. Yes, What light is there outside the birdcage at that hour?

A. It is quite light because there is a light straight opposite.

Q. Is there any street lighting?

A. Yes.

Q. And was it alight?

A. Yes.

Q. What did you see when you went out with Mr Stafford, yourself?

A. I seen where the car had went into the back of his car.

Q. Would you tell the Jury what you saw?

A. When I looked the car had been hit by, you know, it was all battered in, the back.

Mr Raymond Dean cross examined;

Q. You could see quite clearly in the freshly fallen snow, as I understand it, the tracks of another vehicle which apparently had collided with the back of the E-Type and then reversed away, is that right?

A. Yes.

It was actually Matthew Dean who had noticed the other set of tracks to the rear of the E-Type, not Dennis Stafford, and it was he who passed comment that they were there, and he was quite certain that a collision had taken place at that spot. Although not overly significant, it is worth noting that Stafford had not locked the E-Type. It had been targeted by thieves in the past by cutting a hole in the canvas roof so he had decided that leaving it unlocked was a safer option. Photographs of the damage to the E-Type show that the damage was relatively superficial when you consider the far more substantial damage done to the Mark X, a very solidly built Jaguar car. The rear of the E-type is a hollow 'bubble', the front of the Mark X has a steel pillar and is far more robust. Would the E-Type not have incurred far more severe damage?

The apparent minor damage to the E-Type Jaguar

Chapter 5
Guilty Until Proven Guilty

*'…and although this is a fight I could lose, the accused
is an innocent man.' Billy Joel (Innocent man)*

The scene of the murder was now swarming
with police. At 6am Ronald Kell arrived, he took
charge of the investigation. Powerful spotlights lit
up the area around the Mark X Jaguar, and the
roads in the immediate area were sealed off from
the public. The breakdown truck that had been
called to remove the car, with the body still inside,
took two hours to make the four mile journey.
More pictures were taken by the police before the
body was carefully removed from the car wrapped
in polythene sheets, then transferred to Easington
mortuary. The body was laid onto the lead covered
table in a temperature of 28 degrees and the
clothing removed. The post mortem commenced at
1.15pm, the rectal temperature of the body was 64
degrees F. The limbs were now stiffened by rigor
mortis. The examination revealed there were
abrasions to both knees and the left ankle, and
there were scratches to the upper left area of the
abdomen, and further abrasions to the forehead.

Dr Ennis took samples of blood, urine, hair,
and contents of the stomach which were taken to
the northern forensic laboratories in Newcastle

The clothing showed the following;

A. A simple bullet hole through the overcoat, the jacket plus the shirt and braces, behind the left shoulder between the neck and shoulder seam.

B. A simple hole showing a downward direction through the right front of the overcoat, the jacket, the shirt and the vest. About central between the shoulder and waist.

C. A simple hole through both the outer and inner aspects of the right cuff.

D. A complex hole which is represented in the right front chest region, distinctly lower than B, it shows a deeply descending path which shows that the clothing must have been very deranged.

The clothing was also smeared in mud or soil. The overcoat was stained with wet mud, especially the sleeves and left side of the shirt. The trousers had heavy wet mud from the waist to the right thigh, there was no staining at the knee areas. The shirt was quite heavily stained, again with wet mud. The shoes showed light scuff marks on the toes and the left heel had an unexplained, impact damage. The patterns were consistent with the body being dragged both feet first, and head first.

Black residue was found around two of the bullet holes, one frontal and the other rear, at the shoulder, this according to the ballistics expert, Mr George Price, suggested that these two shots were fired at point blank range, possibly as close as half an inch. The third shot he estimated to have been fired from approximately three feet. Mr Norman Lee identified the gun that had been used was a 7.65mm calibre, most likely to be a self loading pistol. The two bullets present in the car were confirmed to be from the same weapon, one in the rear pillar of the rear off-side door which due to residue around the point of entry was assessed to have been fired from a very close range. The second which was found to the rear of the driver's seat, there was no residue and this bullet had also shattered the rear off-side window. Mr Lee later examined the interior of the Mark X Jaguar, where it was being stored in the police yard. Lab tests were also carried out on sweepings from the carpeting and upholstery of the vehicle.

At 'Roker Car Sprays' in Sunderland, the police entered the premises and ordered that the E-type Jaguar be seized, it was kept under police guard, until the recovery to the police yard was carried out. No work had been carried out on the car by the garage since it was admitted. Over the following weeks police officers, cadets and soldiers carried out a search of the scene of the murder, some of which involved the use of metal detectors. Again, the gun was never recovered. A sign bearing the heading; MURDER! was put up around the South Hetton area, appealing for anybody with information, no matter how trivial, to come forward. One of the first was Nora Burnip, a farmer's wife from West Moor Farm. On the 5th of January at 12.20am, she was sharply awakened by the sound of two loud cracks. She was adamant about the time because she looked at the clock as she got out of her bed to look through the window. She saw nothing on the A182, however, a large portion of her view was obscured by a haystack.

The search continued on the A182 and onto Pesspool Lane, it was here that a Detective Constable named Tipler joined the search party, and where he would have what appears to be astounding good luck. On the 7th of January Tipler discovered fragments of Perspex, both red and orange pieces, along with a reflector and some discarded cigarette ends. It is worth noting that the brand of cigarettes identified by the stubs was not the brand smoked by Sibbet, Stafford or Luvaglio. Two days later, and with a totally different search party on the A182 approximately a quarter mile east of South Hetton, Tipler found pieces of glass and more red and orange pieces of Perspex. The following day, yet again, amazingly, Lady luck smiled on DC Tipler, he now found a pair of spectacles and then again on the 10th, he would strike 'lucky' again. He found fragments of glass and two sets of paint fragments, one green and one red. On the other side of the road, on the nine inch kerb he found the two bullet casings from the remaining gunshots. At this point I need to point out another strange discovery, and again this wasn't given in evidence. Forensic analysis of glass and

Perspex fragments found at the scene of the murder showed that neither belonged to a Mark X, or an E-Type Jaguar. Why wasn't it investigated as to what type of car they did belong to?

On the 6th of January DC Richardson entered the Zip Cleaners Company, and retrieved two suits and six shirts belonging to Stafford and Luvaglio, along with many other items of the pair's clothing. Mr Lee again examined these items at Northern Forensic Laboratories, along with the blood stained piece from the telephone directory in the call box where Tom Leak had contacted the police. Sibbet's self promotion that portrayed him as a leading figure in the gambling world must have had an effect, the headline in the local newspaper read, *'Men accused of gaming boss murder'.*

Even though solicitors for both of the accused, argued that there was no solid evidence, i.e. forensics, not even the gun, it was decided anyway that the case was going to Northumberland assizes, sitting at the Moot Hall in Newcastle there would be a trial by jury.

The prosecution stood fast by their theory, that the two accused had committed the murder of Sibbet. They offered no motive other than Mr Scott's statement that *'For some reason Sibbet's presence was no longer desired on this earth. So, he was killed.'* Their theory was based on the following opinions; Stafford and Luvaglio left Westmorland Rise, Peterlee at 11pm, they met Sibbet on the A182,he was driving alone having left the Dolce Vita in

Newcastle. Then they claim that one of the two accused got into the car with Sibbet and followed the E-Type towards South Hetton, where they assumed a collision between the two cars took place. Then they have Sibbet getting out of the car where he was shot at five times. However two shots missed him and hit the car. Then Stafford and Luvaglio supposedly bundled the large man into the back of the Mark X, then both cars were driven away, turning right into Pesspool Lane where they stopped a few hundred yards along the way, supposedly to clean up the mess. They then supposedly drove along the lane, through Haswell village and back to the A182 and headed back through South Hetton, where the Mark X apparently overheated due to a puncture in the radiator, and broke down just prior to the bridge. The men then in a state of panic supposedly abandoned the Mark X leaving the lights on and windshield wipers running, got into the E-type and headed to Newcastle at speed to obtain an alibi. Initially, four witnesses were called by the prosecution, Joseph Knight, Henry Johnson, William Sanderson and James Golden.

Standing in the witness box, Joseph Knight answered questions put to him by Mr Castle-Miller.

Q. Were you able to recognise the makes of the two cars?

A. Well, I thought at the time that the first car was an E-Type Jaguar, and I was sure that the second was a Mark X Jaguar.

Q. Did you happen to notice any part of the registration plate or number on the Mark X?

A. I did notice that the number ended with a D.

Mr Justice O Conner asked;

Q. Well, you saw them pull out, Mr Knight, and that the front one was, you thought, an E-Type, the leading car?

A. Correct, yes.

Q. And there was a Mark X behind that?

A. Yes

Q. They pulled out, and turned in which direction?

A. Towards Easington Lane.

Q. The same way you were going?

A. Yes.

Mr Castle-Miller continued;

Q. Did the Mark X present its back to you as it drove off?

A. That's right.

Q. And was it on the back number plate that you thought you saw the letter D?

A. I did see it, yes.

Q. You did see it? Yes. What sort of speed were they making?

A. Just below thirty mph.

Q. How close were they driving, how close was the front of the Mark X to the back of the E-type?

A. They were very close. I would not like to say because being behind them I could not ascertain this very well.

Q. Did you wait for them to come out across your bows as it were?

A. Oh no, they came out as I was approaching.

Q. Did you have to check speed for them?

A. Er, no. Though, with them pulling out at a slow speed which they did, I eventually caught up with them within a short distance.

Q. You caught up with them, over what distance did you follow them?

A. Approximately half a mile.

Q. And what speed were you all keeping?

A. Just below thirty mph.

Q. How close were you to the Mark X?

A. Two or three yards.

Q. You closed up on it did you?

A. Oh yes.

Q. Did you overtake them?

A. Yes.

Q Where was that?

A. It was a point at a place near the picture house called the 'cozy' in Easington Lane where the road widens.

Q. Is that in Easington Lane?

A. Yes, it is.

Q. And when you came to a junction called the Snippersgate, which way did you turn?

A. I turned right, onto the B1280 to Haswell.

Q. Did you ever see the two vehicles again?

A. Only after I turned around. For curiosity's sake I looked in my rear view mirror to see if, in fact, the first car was an E-Type Jaguar because I had not been too sure prior to that time.

Q. And was it?

A. In my opinion it was.

Then Mr Henry Johnson was called, he had left work at the pit baths at 11.42 and walked to the main road.

Mr Henry Scott asked him;

Q. And did you notice anything as you were standing there waiting for your bus?

A. I noticed two cars pass me.

Q. What make were they?

A. The first one was a red E-Type Jaguar.

Q. And the second?

A. A dark coloured Jaguar, saloon.

Q. What time would that be Mr Johnson?

A. Fourteen minutes to midnight.

Q. How do you know that, it is a rather exact time?

A. After they passed me I looked at my watch to see what time it was for my bus.

Q. And your watch is right is it?

A. Yes sir.

Q. How fast were those cars going?

A. Twenty five to thirty miles an hour.

Q. How far apart were they?

A. No more than five yards.

Q. And were they going in the direction of Easington?

A. Yes sir.

Q. Could you see how many people there were in them?

A. There was one person in the first car.

Q. In the E-Type?

A. Yes, and there was two in the saloon.

The third witness to be called by the prosecution, William Sanderson had been walking with his friend William Cook towards Easington Lane, after finishing their shift at work. They were passing the Bridge Inn, twenty yards before the bridge. He told the prosecution that two cars had passed them in the same direction they were walking, the first an E-Type Jaguar and the second a Jaguar saloon. Mr Castle Miller asked;

Q. Are you able to tell the court what colour either of these cars was?

A. Well, the first one as it went under the light on the south side of the bridge, I noticed was a reddish colour. The second was a darker colour, I couldn't say what colour it was.

Then James Golden was called to the stand, he was cycling along the A182 towards Easington. At 11.50 he reached a walled farm known to locals as Junction House. Mr Scott asked him;

Q. As you cycled along, do you remember anything happening?

A. Just the two cars passing me sir.

Q. That is what I want to ask you about. What sort of cars were they?

A. Two Jaguars sir.

Q. What type of Jaguars were they?

A. One was a sports, E-Type; the other one was a saloon.

Q. Which order were they in?

A. The sports car was in front.

Q. What speed were they going?

A. Probably about sixty mph.

The prosecution now assumed that the collision had occurred outside of West Moor farm, this fell into place with the discovery of Sibbet's glasses, the bullet casings and the Perspex splinters that had been found at this spot. Even though a ballistics expert refutes this due to the way in which spent bullet casings are discharged from the gun, he claims it is more likely the casings were placed there, and this being the case, is it also possible that Sibbet's spectacles were also placed there?

Chapter 6
Evidently Misted

The Police simulated the drive that they alleged the accused had driven. The reason for this was that the defence had argued the timing would simply not be enough to make the journey the two accused had apparently made, in the given time frame. They used the same route as was being alleged. The two detectives who carried out this test run were, Detective Superintendant Arthur Chapman and Detective Superintendant Collinson.

Henry Scott asked;

Q. Starting from Four Lane Ends at Hetton-Le-Hole, that is the junction of the B1284 at the A182, did you start a journey in that car (A mark ten Jaguar)?

A. Yes sir.

Q. And did you travel via Easington Lane, South Hetton, Pesspool Bridge, the A182, Pesspool Lane, Haswell and back to Pesspool Bridge, South Hetton?

A. Yes. Sir.

Q. Did you stop on that journey?

A. Yes, Sir.

Q. Where did you stop the first time?

A. I stopped at a point along the A182 road.

Q. Was that a stop indicated to you by another officer?

A. It was.

Q. Who was that, Superintendant Collinson?

A. It was.

Q. How long did you stop there for?

A. Four minutes.

Q. Four minutes, did you then drive to Pesspool Lane?

A. Yes, Sir.

Q. Did you stop there?

A. Yes Sir, for three minutes.

Q. For three minutes, Superintendant, at a point about 350 yards?

A. Inside the lane towards Haswell.

Q. Then did you travel, well then, of course you went back to Pesspool Bridge. Did you stop when you got to Pesspool Bridge?

A. Yes Sir.

Q. For how long?

A. A matter of roughly about two minutes.

Q. And then what did you do?

A. Turned the car around and travelled from Pesspool Bridge to the Birdcage Club in Newcastle travelling via South Hetton.

They claim to have stuck to the speed limits, driving via Fencehouses, Lambton, Chester-Le Street and onto the A1, through Gateshead and onto Newcastle via the High Level Bridge.

He continued:

Q. Now, what time of day was it that you did that?

A. We started the journey at Four Lane Ends at Hetton-Le-Hole at 11.44 and 30 seconds pm.

Q. At what time did you arrive at the Birdcage Club?

A. About 12.31.

Now, when this test run was carried out, the road conditions were apparently excellent, on the night of the murder the conditions were wet and snowy. Although it was argued that the E-Type Jaguar could have done the journey faster, this does not explain the fact that the two men arrived at the club immaculately dressed and clean, after what they were alleged to have carried out, nor that they did not appear in any way nervous or anxious.

The officers allowed four minutes at the scene of the murder, do they estimate this to be adequate time to carry out the alleged offence? Bearing in mind the bullet casings were supposedly found on the opposite side of the road, we are to believe in four short minutes a man fled his car, was shot dead, and bundled into the back of his car (Not depositing any blood onto the killers!)

At this point Raymond Dean, Luvaglio's defence counsel asked:

Q. Allowing four minutes for the commission of the offence?

A. I do not agree that I allowed four minutes for the commission of the offence. I stopped there for four minutes.

Then Mr Justice O'Connor continued:

Q. This is the time you allowed on your journey, assuming the man had been pulled out of the car and shot on the spot?

Dean interjected:

Q. And put back again?

O'Connor continued:

Q. That is right is it not?

A. Yes sir, I accept that.

Now I must reiterate the evidence provided by Police officers Kell, and Mitchell claiming that both defendants stated that they had left the Peterlee flat at 11pm, which both men, and their legal representatives emphatically deny. Maybe 11.30 would have been an inconvenient time for the prosecution what with the abundance of proof that the men arrived at the Birdcage Club by 12.30. It should also be mentioned that Newcastle solicitor, Harry Mincof who for a time represented Michael Luvaglio states that Kell told him that he knew that Luvaglio was innocent, and that they only want him to say he left Stafford for an hour and they would let him go. Of course, Kell vigorously denies this. Mincof added that he can usually ascertain quickly if somebody he is representing is actually guilty, he never once believed that Luvaglio was anything other than innocent.

Now, between 12.30am and 1am three men with no connection to each other drove along the A182 at varying times and passed the abandoned Mark X. The first was farmer, Mr Sidney Lee who passed the car at 12.35, on his way to Easington Lane, he stated that there was nobody either in the car or standing near it, he does however, remember the lights were on. Then the second man, van driver, Mr Clifford Miller from West Hartlepool passed at 12.45, he also noticed that the lights were on and also added that the driver's window was open. The third witness was livestock transporter, Reuben Conroy who was travelling on the same road but in the opposite direction to the other two men. He passed the car at 12.50am, he also noticed that the lights were on but also noticed the windscreen wipers were running. It seems strange that none of these three men reported seeing any damage to the car at this time, a time that we know to be fact, that Dennis Stafford and Michael Luvaglio were seventeen miles away in the Birdcage Club.

Dr Ennis while standing in the witness box gave his version of events that had 'probably' happened that night.

"I visualise that the deceased had opened the car door and was emerging, holding the door still with his left hand and his right hand somewhat against the right hand side of the abutment and the first injury he would then receive was the one which passed through the right, lower forearm and through the right loin tissues. I visualise, then, that he ducked and in the course of ducking and stooping he then received a second wound, probably the one on the left. Behind the left shoulder followed very quickly by the third one on the lower chest. He then falls forward onto his face and onto his hands and the front part of his body. Ennis did admit however that this was speculative, and only his opinion. Again, I reiterate that there was no forensic evidence linking the two accused men with the crime, no blood from the gunshots or from dragging the body and bundling it into the car, no dirt or grass remnants on the accused clothing and no weapon. The internationally recognised expert on medical jurisprudence, Professor John Glaister who had over forty years of experience states in his book, 'Final Diagnosis', "In simple terms, it is almost impossible for anybody to go to the scene of a crime without either leaving some trace of his visit behind him, or carrying away, all unsuspectingly, some trace which links him with the place. Surely to find two men guilty *'Beyond a reasonable doubt'* should have required more than guesswork, speculation and circumstantial conjecture. It should also be noted here, that Ennis had estimated when assessing the time of Sibbet's death, that the body's cooling time would have been slowed down by the heater running in the

Jaguar after it had supposedly broken down, he stated that he believed it would have kept warm air blowing into the car for half an hour. A Jaguar car expert, Mr Sunter, was called to give a statement; he said it would have been *one minute* at the most. Sibbet's hair and beard had un-melted snow on them, surely this would point to the heat in the car being too low to claim that the heater was working, also even interior heat would cause snow to gradually melt from its windows or roof, why were they covered in snow? Another expert stated that the damage to the E-Type Jaguar's rear lights could not have been caused solely by a collision and that some of the damage was most definitely caused by the car being hit maliciously, by a hammer for example. Ennis never accurately took the weight of Sibbet, he merely estimated his weight, why is this relevant? Well, body weight is a very influencing factor in the time a body takes to cool, post mortem. When asked about the fatal wound, Ennis when asked by Mr Scott, how long Sibbet would have been alive after the bullet through the shoulder, that obliterated many vital organs was fired, replied, "Not more than a minute".

So, by the prosecution's theory on what had occurred, body cooling would have initialised immediately (which according to them was before midnight). Ennis had initially given time of death to be within a four hour threshold, however, when pressed he said he would estimate 12am, quite convenient that his change of story should fit in with the prosecution's theory. When pressed further by Mr Scott, the following was said;

Q. And if you say, well, of the four hours I prefer the first two, does not that make it more likely that taking two single hours, twelve to one; one to two; it is more likely that it was one to two than twelve to one?

A. No, I prefer...

Q. You prefer twelve to one?

A. Yes.

Q. Would half past twelve be a reasonable time?

A. Yes.

Q. Twenty past twelve?

A. Yes.

Q. More likely twenty past twelve or half past twelve than before twelve?

A. I would not argue that it could not have occurred a short time before twelve.

Q. That is not what I am asking you, we are going on probabilities.

A. We cannot be precise in stating a time.

There were some microscopic flecks of red paint found in the pocket of one of Stafford's suits that had been retrieved from Zip Cleaners, he explained this by stating that he had examined the damage to the E-Type and then the suit was one of the items he had placed in the boot on January the 6th, Detective Sergeant Morgan stated, in the witness box, that this was perfectly plausible.

Mr. Lyons quizzed the forensics expert Mr. Lee further, about his findings on the clothes belonging to Michael Luvaglio and Dennis Stafford;

Q. Did you find any grass debris on the clothing of Mr Stafford?

A. No sir.

Q. Or Mr Luvaglio?

A. No sir.

Q. Perhaps I ought to mention as it is grass debris, the shoes. You examined quite a number of shoes belonging to Mr Stafford?

A. Yes.

Q. Did you find any on his shoes?

A. No, sir.

Q. The ladies on the jury will know how easy it is to carry grass debris onto the carpet of a room in the house; grass debris could be carried on a shoe anywhere?

A. Yes, it could.

Q. And deposited by that shoe?

A. Yes.

Q. Did you find any grass debris in the E-Type Jaguar?

A. No, Sir.

Again, just like Sibbet's blood, the dirt, the grass and soaking wet snow that would have been in abundance while the act of murder took place, we are to believe that the two defendants managed, in the dark of night, to leave at speed in a less than inconspicuous car like an E-Type, without being even slightly contaminated by the bleeding body that had been shot three times or the surroundings at the scene of the murder, and not even trail any dirt into the car, or onto their clothes?

The fact that Sibbet's blood was found in the telephone kiosk would have surely warranted a fingerprinting examination of the coins in the coin box of the kiosk? Why did this not take place?

For the impact marks of the exhaust pipe on the E-Type to have hit the number plate of the Mark X, the rear end of the E-Type would have had to be pushed in a further four inches, otherwise, it could not have happened, so how did the mark appear? For the perfect circle that the prosecution claimed was a result of a collision between the two vehicles, they would have needed a straight-on crash otherwise it would have been a crescent shaped mark, well, if it were head on why is there not a second circle being as the E-Type has a twin exhaust?

Renowned Pathologist, Francis Comps, took a close look at the evidence and at the testimony of Dr Ennis. He looked perplexed by the outcome and stated, "There was simply not adequate evidence to convict these two men".

Chapter 7

Can I Get A Witness

In this chapter I want to take a more in-depth look into the witnesses who the prosecution tried to avoid calling to the stand, and the ones who they succeeded in keeping out of the whole trial. I was quite amazed to discover that there were actually one hundred and sixty four, omissions that included fingerprint evidence, and statement changes that were not admitted to the court. I will now reveal a section of the suppressed evidence.

I will first mention Tom Leak, the man who discovered the body at 5.15am on January 5th, now then, as I stated earlier this man was only called to give evidence due to the insistence of Stafford's legal representative. Leak was a man with a responsible position dealing with explosives on the coal seams, his lack of judgement could have caused a disaster. His testimony was called into question about the position of Sibbet's leg, maybe it wasn't desired information.

11:50pm - P.C. Grierson & P.C. Hafferty: written statements swearing that the road was deserted, and there were no other cars travelling in the opposite direction to them in South Hetton at that time.

12:10am - Mauro Terry: saw no motor vehicle

stationary under or near Pesspool Bridge at that time.

12:20am - P.C. Ainsworth saw a Mark X Jaguar and a Red Mini pass them (FACT: the paint and undercoat layers from a red Mini are exactly the same as the paint and undercoat layers of a Red E-Type).

12:30 am- Mr. Ord saw a dark coloured Mark X under Pesspool Bridge (not prior to it). He did not see any damage.

12:35am - Mr. Lee saw a Mark X under the bridge - no damage to it.

12:45am - Mr. Miller saw a Mark X under the bridge - no damage to it, no dead body inside it.

12:45am - Mr. McLeall (Bus Driver) saw a Mark X under the bridge - no damage to it.

12:45am - Mr. Forster saw a Mark X under the bridge - no damage to it.

12:47am - Mr. Feather(Bus Driver) saw a Mark X under the bridge and an arm that came out of the driver's window and giving him the overtake signal. At this time the Prosecution claim that only a dead body was in the car, not a live one. Undisputed fact at this time is that Stafford and Luvaglio were at the Bird Cage Club in Newcastle 17 miles away.

12:55am - Mr. Conroy saw a Mark X under the bridge - "At the time when I passed the vehicle I am certain that if that vehicle had been damaged I would have noticed it." He also did not notice anyone in the car.

1:07am - Mr. & Mrs. Robinson passed the Mark X under the bridge on the same side of the road but it was facing the wrong way. It had been completely turned around. They were astounded to see the front of a Mark X Jaguar facing them. "We slowed down at this point thinking someone may be in trouble." Mr. Robinson had his headlights on, and there was definitely no damage to the front of the car, all the windows were intact. The front and rear seats were completely empty. There was definitely no body in the car.

1:10am - Mr. Sturrock saw a Mark X just before the bridge - "This car was parked at an acute angle to the kerb -- the interior light was on." (The Mark X was in the process of being turned around)

1:12am - Mr. Johnson saw a Mark X "S" type (different model to Angus's Mark X) parked just prior to the bridge. (The Mark X had been facing the other way at this point and nearly back into its position under the bridge)

1:15am - Mr McLeall (Bus Driver) passed the Mark X again under the bridge. He had his headlights on which flood lit the front of the car and it was still not damaged at this point.

1:30am - Mr. Gibson did not see any cars at all parked near to or under the bridge. The Mark X was not there at all!

1:40am - Mr. Wilson saw a Mark X under the bridge. There was no damage to the front of the car and the rear offside window was intact.

1:40am - Mr. Sutton saw a Mark X under the bridge. There was no damage to the front of the car and the rear offside window was intact.

1:50am - Mr. Wood saw a Mark X under the bridge. The passenger front and rear doors were open, there were pointed toe shoe prints in the snow leading away from car (miners wore work boots not pointed toe shoes). At the time the police claimed the murder was committed, it wasn't snowing, so how could the footprints be those of Luvaglio or Stafford when they were in the Bird Cage Club from 12:30 onwards? There was no damage to the front of the car (Mr. Wood was standing 2 inches away from it. He opened the passenger door fully. The rear was completely empty, no body on the back seat and all windows were intact. Why didn't the police find Mr Woods fingerprints on the Mark X while it was in their custody at the Police Yard? This makes the likelihood of a second Jaguar plausible.

1:55am - Mr McLelement passed the Mark X under the bridge. He had his headlights on and noticed no damage to the car, no body in it either.

2:00am - Jean Turnbull saw a Mark X under the bridge. There was no damage to the car.

2:00am - Mr Whorton saw a Mark X under the bridge. There was no damage to the car, no dead body inside the car.

2:20am - Mr Bradbury saw a Mark X under the

bridge. He walked around the car several times. There was definitely no damage to the front of the car and the rear offside window was intact. He looked in all windows and there was definitely no body inside the car, it was completely empty. He put his hand on the bonnet of the car to lean over and look inside through the windscreen. He did not feel or see any damage to the bonnet. The police took fingerprints from the Mark X while in their custody. Why weren't Mr. Bradbury's fingerprints and palm prints found on the bonnet of the car they had in custody? Once more the likelihood of a second Jaguar being involved in this murder case is plausible.

2:25am Mr. Purvis, Mr. Simpson and Mr. Howie all saw an undamaged Mark X under the bridge. Mr. Purvis and Mr. Simpson walked around the offside of the car. All the windows were intact and there was no body inside the car. Mr. Simpson felt the front offside headlamp of the car with his hand. It was not broken (the Mark X the police had, had a broken offside headlamp). He then ran his hand along the entire length of the Mark X. Mr. Simpson's fingerprints and palm prints were not found on the Mark X the police had (his fingerprints weren't found because the car in police custody wasn't the car he touched). Mr. Howie examined the car carefully. He was a professional driver. There was definitely no damage to the front of the car. He looked inside. The car was completely empty and there was definitely no body inside the car.

2:35am - Mr Joshua Leek saw a Mark X under the bridge. There was no damage and no body inside it.

2:40am - Mr Quinn saw a Mark X under the bridge. There was no damage to the car.

2:40am - Mr Kitchling saw a Mark X under the bridge. There was no damage to the car.

2:55am - Mr Rutter saw a Mark X under the bridge. There was no damage to the car.

2:55am - Mr Wilson saw a Mark X under the bridge. There was no damage to the car.

3:00am - Mr Oliver saw a Mark X under the bridge. There was no damage to the car.

3:20am - Mr Pickering saw a Mark X under the bridge. There was no damage to the car.

3:30am - Mr Hathaway saw a Mark X under the bridge. There was no damage to the car and no body inside it.

3:30am - Mr Wallace saw a Mark X under the bridge. There was no damage.

3:30am - Mr Johnson saw a Mark X under the bridge. It was definitely not damaged - "The car headlights were on and in that photograph the car has a damaged headlight"....."I bent down to look inside the car. The car was completely empty". There was no body inside the car and the windows were intact.

3:40am - Mr England saw a Mark X under the bridge. It was definitely not damaged.

4:45am - Mr King saw a Mark X under the bridge. It was definitely not damaged and the windows were intact.

4:50am - Mr Brodighm saw no Mark X under, or near to the bridge. The only car in the vicinity was a cream-coloured Vauxhall Victor.

5:15am - Mr Leak found a Mark X Jaguar parked just prior to Pesspool Bridge. (not under the bridge) The front of the car was smashed in, the rear offside window was shot out and Angus's dead body was partially propped up on the rear seat. Tom Leak was the first miner to discover the body. When he opened the door he saw Angus Sibbett lying on the back seat with his left leg lying on the seat and his right leg was hanging down to the floor. He shook his trouser leg thinking he was asleep and said "you can't park here mate". This is when he realized that Angus was dead. He left the body and on the way to the phone booth to call the police, he met the other men who then went and looked for themselves. At a later date when Mr. Leak saw the police photograph of Angus in the back seat of the car, Angus's right leg was not hanging over the edge of the seat and down to the floor, it was bent with the left leg and both legs were leaning on the backseat. A big part of the investigation was determining the time of death. This would have been established by being able to determine when rigor mortis had set in. If a corpse is moved when rigor mortis has already set in, it breaks the rigor mortis and it then becomes impossible to determine an accurate time of death. Since someone had changed the position of the legs, it was no longer possible to determine an accurate time of death. Who moved Angus's leg and why?

Mr. Wallace (3:30am) on being questioned in court in 1972 and on being shown the police photographs of a Mark X parked just prior to Pesspool Bridge stated "If you park another Mark X in front of that one in the photograph, that is the position I saw a Mark X under the bridge. The contradiction here is in the position of the car under Pesspool Bridge as shown in the photo provided by police when Angus was found dead in his Mark X at 5:15am and the position that thirty five witnesses saw it in between 12:30am and 4:45am being the length of another Mark X Jaguar.

The police did not find the fingerprints and palm prints of Mr. Woods, Mr. Bradbury and Mr. Simpson on the Mark X they had in their possession.

Thirty five of the above witnesses saw an undamaged Mark X with no body in it. The Lord Chief Justice and five Law Lords said that although all these witnesses were honest and reliable, they must have been mistaken. How is it possible that all of these witnesses be mistaken?

Not one witness saw a damaged Mark X Jaguar

with the two offside windows shot out and Angus's murdered body on the back seat of the car until it was found in that condition at 5:15am by Tom Leak.

All of the above, is only a selection of witness evidence, not shown to the jury who, let's not forget, were there to establish, using *all available* evidence, beyond reasonable doubt, the guilt of the two accused men.

Another important point to note here is the witness testimony that also has Sibbet leaving the Dolce Vita club at 11.20pm to 11.30pm this would also mean that he would have had to arrive at the place of his death just as rapidly as we are to believe the two accused made the journey in the other direction. We are then to presume that even by Dr Eniss's farfetched timing of events, which scientifically do not hold any level of being convincing, that Sibbet was killed virtually bang on midnight, and let's not forget, his initial estimate was 12am to 4am which he only changed when apparently pressed to do so. If Sibbet had driven to suit the conditions and within speed limits and we assume the two accused men adopted the same principal, then realistically Sibbet would not have arrived at South Hetton until approximately 12.15, which would then mean, that even if Sibbet was killed straight away, and the accused hadn't taken that detour around Pesspool Lane (Which they would have had to have done for the Mark X to be abandoned where it was), and then if we presume that they managed to scrub all traces of forensic evidence from themselves and of course the E-Type Jaguar (Virtually an impossible feat forensically speaking), that they arrived at the Birdcage Club, calm and clean and at 12.30 which is substantiated by witnesses, which now puts the time it took to get to the Birdcage Club at fifteen minutes. That is fifteen minutes to Shoot a man dead, bundle his heavily built dead body into the back of a car, drive off-road to clean yourself and your clothes, drive seventeen miles and enter a nightclub showing no signs of anxiety. Does this sound feasible to you? It appears to me that the times have been bent and twisted into the shape that was needed to fit the puzzle, and basic truths have been overlooked.

Chapter 8
Caesar's Fall

Tuesday the 14th of March, Mr Justice O'Connor was ready to sum up the six day trial. The people in the court, the press and observers from the general public were all geared up for the verdict. The vast majority thinking there was only one outcome that would be reached, the men would be acquitted. Even bookmakers were taking bets on the outcome, odds strongly in favour (for the bookmaker) of the men being found innocent. However, by the time the jury retired the odds took a reversal. Mr Justice O'Connor expressed to the jury that if they were under the impression that he was trying to guide them in any direction with regard to evidence heard, that they should disregard it. This would already sway the average person, who would see a man of such high standing and intelligence as being unlikely to be incorrect in his opinions. While on the subject of potentially swaying the jury, another '*accidental*' slip of the tongue from O'Connor that could have had a negative effect on the jury's opinion of the accused was when he referred to Stafford's return from 'Jamaica' which he swiftly corrected by saying, "Sorry Majorca." Of course this was enough to register in the minds of the jury members with the potential effect of sparking the memory of the very high profile extradition of Stafford from Jamaica, to bring him back to jail after his escape. So much for a jury not having an accused person's background, or past, brought to their attention.

He then referred to the backgrounds of the accused, he stated he understood that certain people may find their lifestyle abhorrent; *It may be repellent to some or all of you, but you are not trying Stafford or Luvaglio for living what some of you may consider a very immoral life. They are not being tried for being unfaithful to their wives or mistresses.* Now then, considering neither Stafford nor Luvaglio were even married, this was hardly a fair picture to paint. He then referred to the activities of Social Club Services Ltd. by stating that their type of business was not desirable in the community. Gambling laws were in place by this time and their business was totally legitimate. O'Conner then asked, *Was there another person in the murdering gang?* Does this not imply that the two men are already guilty? He then decided to adjourn his summing up until the following day, at the time it was confusing as to why he had chosen to do this.

On the 15th of March the summing up reached a new level of drama, or pantomime may be a more appropriate term to describe what was being invoked by O'Connor, *As human beings you will, of course, know that friends are of two types; true friends and false friends. Today is the exact anniversary of the uttering of the famous cry which has rung down through the ages when Julius Caesar lay dying. 'And you Brutus,' whose dagger was in his heart. His friend. Seventy five years later one greater than Caesar was betrayed by Judas with a kiss. You have seen and heard Michael Luvaglio give his evidence. Is he a good actor? Was he a true friend or not?'* Very dramatic.. or it could be said, very 'convenient'. If O'Connor had actually finished his summing up on the previous day when he had ample time to do so, then the jury would not have been treated to such a performance as the date would not have fit in with this climatic scene. Of course, I am not suggesting that this was the whole reason for the adjournment.

Then Justice O'Connor told the jury, that although they must be sure they have the people responsible before giving a guilty verdict, motive was not fully necessary to establish guilt. What about Norma Burnip's testimony? Well again she was discredited for no apparent reason, *"Mrs. Burnip's recollection you may think, is based on her normal habits and you may think that she may be a long time out in her recollection. You have seen and heard the lady give her evidence, because it could be that lights were put out quite a long time earlier and that really, her recollection is that it was about twenty minutes after the lights were put out, whenever that was, that she heard the cracks. She said that her recollection, to the best of her recollection that is, that the lights were put out around midnight, but you see, you may think that it is again the type of recollection as to time which is based on an uncertain start, and it may be that she is up to half an hour out. If one has gone to bed at half past nine would you accurately remember if you had read for two hours or two and a half hours?"* It was clear what the opinion of Justice O'Connor was without him spelling it out. Nora Burnip was exact in her time, she didn't say 'approximately' or 'between' she said categorically, 12.20am. Why throw doubt on her testimony? And Mr Feather, a competent and professional driver, he saw a hand coming out of the car and either waving him past or flagging him down, this was put down to bad lighting. And then another example of wording that by some could be interpreted as leading the jury, the judge said, 'maybe there was the dead man, and *another* man in the car'. Well, at that time there was no solid proof that Sibbet was actually dead other than the theories of the prosecution on which no verdict had been reached. Witnesses who claim to have seen the two Jaguars in tandem state that there was only three men altogether, if there were a fourth where was he? The E-Type Jaguar is a two seated car. Dorothy Brady stated that she saw the E-type Jaguar outside of the Birdcage Club when she arrived there, then noticed it was gone when she left. Stafford and Luvaglio were both in the club the whole time, Matthew Dean the doorman verified that the men had not left.

Now the statements of Selena Jones and Pat Burgess. It can be accepted that these two women had reason to defend the two men unlike the rest of the witnesses, the fact that they said the two men had left the Peterlee flat at 11.30pm, according to Detective Kell who was adamant the men had stated that they had left at 11.00pm, albeit that this was vigorously denied by Stafford, Luvaglio and Stafford's solicitor. Then we have to assume that either both men and the two women did not concoct an alibi as the timing would have been paramount in the conspiracy, or the accused men actually said 11.30pm as they claim to have done. In which case if they were trying to build an alibi, surely they would have done so in such a way as to alter the timing far more significantly?

The damage to the Mark X's radiator was not consistent with being caused by collision. Car expert Mr. A.G.F. Bowman stated that it was more likely to have been stabbed with a screwdriver or something similar, and in another twist on the 25th April 1973 an anonymous letter was received by the Registrar of Criminal Appeals which read as follows;

'I have no idea if this information is of any significance but I feel like the solicitors of Dennis Stafford and Michael Luvaglio should be informed. On the 7th of January 1967, Frank Morgan ran the engine of the Mark X without water which would give the impression of overheating. This occurred in the station yard Peterlee. I am confident that Mac noticed the difference of engine condition on a later inspection of the vehicle in question. With a family to consider it is obvious that I can't put my name to this letter, but I swear it is the truth, and a few inquiries will reveal that this is common knowledge. For Justice.' My research suggests Mac refers to PC McQueen whose report read, *'engine started, good mechanical order'*

If the men were implicated in the murder, and

if opinions are that they were behind it, if not directly involved then this raises a question in my mind. Why, if there was any connection with Stafford and Luvaglio and the murder, would the men be so heavily implicated in the whole affair, when they could have built themselves a cast iron alibi by being somewhere with a host of witnesses for the whole night, or even remained in Majorca till the act was carried out. Hence, distancing them from the matter without being anywhere close to the North East? The only answer in my mind is that they were totally unaware of what was going to take place.

I also then need to question something else that doesn't make sense to me. If the two men were the ruthless killers that we are supposed to believe they are, then why was the execution so public? The men were friends. And, even if you agree with the judge with regard to his '*types of friends*' statement, and, the men were faking their friendship, Sibbet certainly believed the two men to be his friends, hence would have agreed to meet the two men anywhere at any time. He could have been lured to any property, business or commercial that the two accused clearly had access to, and killed without any trace, he would have became a missing person. Why would the two men involve themselves in such a messy affair when they would have had the means to never be implicated?

Chapter 9

Scotch Johnny

I have read endless books, trial transcripts and newspaper articles relating to this case, scoured old newsreels and film archives. The one common denominator is that the majority of those people with knowledge of the case including politicians, police officers, criminals and even people who were simply acquainted with the two men believe that a miscarriage of justice occurred, and that to the best of their knowledge, two innocent men were convicted. Richardson gang member, Frankie Fraser claims to know the identity of the real murderers, one of whom he names, a notorious Scottish gangster now deceased, a man whose trademark killings usually resulted in a bullet ridden body being found in a car. The other, Fraser claims, is still alive so he refuses to name him. Former football club chairman, businessman, and one time safe-cracker George Reynolds stated in an interview that he knows 100% that at least one of the two, and highly likely both men were innocent; the Krays apparently revealed that they had killed another man, could this have been Sibbet? I personally think that this is unlikely as it was quite widely accepted that a man named Ginger Marks was the man they referred to, but it must also be stated that it is not an impossible scenario that they had a hand in the murder either, in fact it is alleged that the solicitor of Reginald Kray, before he was incarcerated, made Dennis Stafford's solicitor an offer that if he gave him anything that might discredit the police case against his client, then Kray would name the killers of Angus Sibbet, this never happened. An incident that fits in with the theory of a London gang trying to muscle in on the business was when; a twenty six year old company director by the name of Mohamed Avais received a threatening message which was left on his telephone answering machine. He reported the incident to the police, below is a transcript of his written statement;

'I carry on business at the above address as The Northern Auto Machines Company Ltd. My work takes me to many of the nightclubs in the north-east of England and as a representative I meet most club owners. At my business premises I have installed a telephone answering machine which records messages for me at the office. On Friday 6th of January at about 6.15 pm I had occasion to play the machine and there was a message on it for me by someone unknown to me, which read: This is for Mr Avais. You may have read the evening papers. There is something quite interesting. You are next Mr Avais. You are next. This is a well known firm. You will be joining Mr Sibbet very shortly -goodbye. I reported this to the police straight away and still have the tape in my possession. I have handed to police, a recording of the same. Signed Mohamed Avais.

There have been all manner of rumours and Chinese whispers relating to the case, from Vince

Landa, disgruntled girlfriends, wives (and their husbands!) to the Kray twins being implicated. Maybe the truth will never come out, however, as I have already explained, that is not the reason behind this book. I am not looking to point a finger at anybody, I am merely hoping to show the paper thin case that resulted in the convictions of Mr's Stafford and Luvaglio, and in this writers opinion resulted in the wrongful conviction of two men.

I then came across a very curious piece of archive film footage from 1973; it contained a video in which a man by the name of John Tumbelty admitted picking up the alleged real killer from South Hetton on that fateful night. I decided to explore this further.

John Tumbelty, otherwise known as Scotch Johnny was a petty criminal living in Newcastle at the time. He came forward in 1968 while in prison, with a bizarre yet strangely plausible story he felt he needed to tell. He confessed to a fellow inmate that he had driven the real killer of Angus Sibbet to Newcastle that night. Some time after his release, he was tracked down by an investigative journalist, and in 1973 he reluctantly gave an interview with a documentary programme on television. He claims that while in the Birdcage club in the early hours of the 5th of January, at about 1.00am he received a telephone call from a Londoner who was known to him, asking to be picked up on the road leading from South Hetton, and that he would set off in the direction of Newcastle. Matthew Dean the Birdcage doorman corroborates this, he remembers Tumbelty asking if he left for an hour or so, whether he would be allowed back into the club. Throughout the interview he claims that he drove a car to the A182, about a mile from Pesspool bridge, where he picked up the caller. The man had a cut on his left calf and blood was soaking his leg and had seeped onto his foot. He says he didn't ask any questions and that the man said to get him back to Newcastle, to the Birdcage.

Below is a transcript from the interview;

Q. At what time Mr Tumbelty, did you go to the Birdcage Club on the night of January 4th?

A. Well it was after the bars closed, you know, between 10.30 and 11pm, something about that time.

Q. And who was in the club that night?

A. Well, there was a number of faces that I knew; on reflection it's not very easy to remember all of them. Of course, Stafford and Luvaglio were there, there's a few other people that I knew, (Bleeping out of name!) and there was a cockney chap with him who had been around for a few days, of course being a strange face and the company he was keeping, well, it was easy to see he was a stranger, you know.

Q. You got a phone call I believe, at what time was this?

A. The nearest I can place this, and I've thought a lot about this that I can place the telephone call would be between 12 and 1 o clock, I couldn't put it any nearer than that.

Q. Who was it from?

A. Well it was from this cockney chap, I knew from his voice that it was him.

Q. Mr Tumbelty, he knew who you were, are you saying that you didn't know who he was?

A. Well, I recognised his voice, you know, he had a distinctive voice and I recognised it immediately.

Q. And what did he ask you to do?

A. Well he asked me to pick him up, that he was stuck out near South Hetton, he said 'do you know the road' I said yes, he said 'can you get transport' I said I think I can yes. He said 'how soon can you get out here?' I said I'll leave right away. He said 'right, I'll walk towards Newcastle, do you know the road?' I said yes, he told me to keep an eye out for him".

Then he claims that on arrival the Londoner started having a heated row with a man who was also in the club and Tumbelty also knew, (the man was neither Stafford or Luvaglio, however Tumbelty does recall that they were both in the Birdcage at the time) saying words to the effect of, 'You shouldn't have left me you mad bastard!' He then goes on to say that he was called to a meeting a couple of days later at a pub called the Greyhound, with the man who had been arguing with the Londoner who he had picked up, the man said to him, 'You know, I have had to ok you, you know that?' Tumbelty replied, "what do you mean?" the man said, 'Because you went out to pick him up, I had to say that you were ok, you had best forget all about it.' Tumbelty made it clear that he had already forgotten about it. The man went on to tell him that it was a situation that had gone wrong, that a man was brought up from London to scare Sibbet, about what, is speculation, maybe about stealing from his employer, or possibly being coerced by a London firm who maybe tried to make him think that it would be in his interests to try and push their fruit machine businesses into the clubs, where Sibbet knew everybody that was worth knowing. The alleged gunman had supposedly started to act erratically and opened fire, shooting Sibbet, that's why according to the man he fled the scene leaving the shooter there.

The man was tracked down and interviewed, his face blacked out, he denied all knowledge of driving the E-Type that night. However, he did admit that Tumbelty's story could be true, with his name disassociated with it of course. Then he asked a seemingly strange question, 'If Stafford and Luvaglio were to be released from prison, could anybody else stand trial for the murder?' Tumbelty was keeping a calm demeanour throughout the interview, that is, until he was asked about his collection of guns. He went on to tell about how he had many guns that were passed around the criminal fraternity. Then a statement was read to him from a former associate of his, named Andrew Johnson, who claimed that during a get together at his house at Newcastle in February 1967, Tumbelty had told him that he had provided the gun that had been used to kill Sibbet. He looked a little bit agitated at the implication, he then conceded that there was a possibility that the gun used on Sibbet was one of his but if it were the case, he had no knowledge of it. The interviewer then pressed Tumbelty, he asked him, 'Doesn't that explain why you went out there that night to pick up the gunman, because you had provided the gun and feared that you may be implicated in the murder?' Tumbelty paused then replied, "Well if that was the case, I'd hardly be telling you that I went out to pick him up, now would I?" The interviewer added, "So if we were to try and find that gun that was used in Sibbet's murder, we would have to dredge the Tyne would we?" Tumbelty responded, "Yea, there must be ten feet of mud over it now, it was six years ago".

Tumbelty who became a legitimate businessman would later retract his statements, denying everything he had said was true. It is believed widely that this was due to threats he had received.

Chapter 10
Viewpoint

Researching this book has been like wading through treacle, there are so many twists and turns, I compare it to the famous words spoken by Churchill, '*it's a riddle, wrapped in a mystery, surrounded by an enigma'*, When the judge said this was a puzzle that would never be solved as there are too many pieces missing, well, I would have to agree. In this chapter I want to push to the fore, facts that I personally feel are the crux of this whole case.

I will start with motive, none was ever proven. Even had Sibbet been stealing from his employers, which my research suggests is pretty much fact, then considering the options open to them, they could have got the police involved, they could have sacked him, and even if they wanted to teach him a lesson surely he would have gotten a beating rather that an execution. And even if this was the motive for murder, as I stated earlier, surely a man of Landa's means would have used outsiders and not implicated his own brother?

As I stated early in this book, why would the two men be so eager to clear their names after all of this time? They are free men albeit with being on life licence for murder. The two men, especially Michael Luvaglio, are desperate not to die labelled as murderers.

Why were so many witness statements not presented at the trial? Could reasonable doubt have been established if there was not such a selective method of choosing what was admitted to the court? My opinion is yes, absolutely. With such a high number of witnesses who saw the car parked with no apparent damage, several of whom were car enthusiasts who actually studied the car closely, and also let's not forget while they studied the car they didn't notice the fourteen stone body lying across the back seat. Then the bus driver who would be probably a more observant driver than the average person who saw the arm waving him by through the car window, again he was deemed to be mistaken. Why were witnesses who place the accused miles away from the scene of the crime at the time of the murder, disregarded as incompetent or mistaken? As were all witnesses who posed any opposition to the prosecution's case.

Why was there no forensic evidence at all? Any forensics expert will state without exception that this is virtually impossible.

I have to also question whether certain evidence which was discovered at the crime scene like the bullet casings, the car lens fragments and spectacles were there as remnants of the crime or is it possible that they were placed there? I also wonder why a Jaguar expert states that the car was in good mechanical order and although would have knocked loudly it was driveable. Then an anonymous letter which I quoted in an earlier chapter, states that the car was run with the water drained from the radiator in the police yard, and of course there were the two holes in the radiator that were not caused by the collision but by stabbing, not to mention the Jaguar expert testimony that the damage to the lights on the E-Type were consistent with being hit by a hammer rather than by the collision. Why was so much effort made to make the cars appear to have collided?

What about Scotch Johnny? Well, in some quarters it is said of this man, he could be the type of person to try and draw attention to himself, but realistically, why involve himself in such a high profile case that could land him in jail?

Then Dr Ennis's assessment of the time of death, it was largely based on guesswork and conjecture, plus of course the changing testimony of Dr Hunter in which he changed his own initial estimate to suit that of the prosecution, which he based on proven inconsistencies pointed out by a Jaguar engineer relating to the car's heater, and let's not forget his less than precise method of weighing Angus Sibbet, which is crucial to the cooling of a dead body, he guessed! Today this would not be accepted as evidence and would be laughed out of court. A police officer soon after the discovery of Sibbet's body, noted there was fresh blood dripping from a wound on the body, also Mr Marshall, when feeling for a pulse felt warmth from the carotid artery. How could this be possible if the murder had taken place at midnight of the previous evening? This is an extract from PC Cluer's notes; *'Wound right side of body, pool of blood on floor beneath wound which was still dripping. Felt pulse on left arm and felt for heartbeat. No sign.'*

Who did the blood on the transmission tunnel in the Mark X belong to? It is fact that it did not belong to Sibbet, Stafford or Luvaglio.

Why was the police officer who saw fresh blood seeping from a wound on Sibbet's body not called to give evidence? And why were the forty plus witnesses, some of whom had approached the car as enthusiasts and scrutinised it at close range left unheard? I am not suggesting that this was simply because when the witnesses saw the car in perfect condition, without smashed windows and without a fourteen stone corpse in the back seat, that it was because Dennis Stafford and Michael Luvaglio were in the Birdcage Nightclub at the time hence making it impossible for them to have carried out the murder.

And to reiterate the supposed accomplishment of the two men, in the forty five minute timeframe. Sibbet got to the spot where he was killed after leaving Newcastle, even quicker than the accused supposedly got back to Newcastle, some seventeen miles away. They then supposedly shot a man dead, dragged his heavily bleeding body through wet mud, snow and grass, bundled his large frame into the back of his car, drove through a village where workers from the colliery would be going to and coming home from work. They then supposedly abandoned the car and fled to Newcastle at breakneck speed in the E-Type Jaguar through blizzard snow and icy roads; arrive at the Birdcage club, calmly appearing immaculate and clean. Then somehow during all of this extremely busy forty five minutes they managed not to pick up any forensic evidence against them whatsoever on their bodies, their clothes or the car in which they supposedly carried out this act. If this were to be the script of a movie it would be panned as being way too farfetched.

Epilogue

Dennis Stafford and Michael Luvaglio know that the time to clear their names is running out. Stafford is now retired after running several legitimate businesses since his release although he has since his release fallen foul of the law for forging traveller's cheques and a more minor shoplifting charge. His Father Joe Stafford handed in a petition to the establishment, a great number of people supported the theory that there had been a serious miscarriage of justice, it fell on deaf ears. Michael Luvaglio couldn't face returning to the north-east, he settled back in London, where for over thirty years he worked for charities who provide help to the mentally and physically disabled, for which he has been commended for his work. He claims the police told him he would walk away a free man if he simply stated that Stafford had left him at some point on that fateful night, as a man of honour and integrity he refused to accept this as he would not entertain lying to save himself. In 1987 during a television programme about the case he could not contain tears as he visited Sibbet's grave. To this day he maintains that he loved Sibbet like a brother and that he was his best friend, there is no evidence to suggest that this was not the case. During the programme as he looked pensively at photographs of the Mark X Jaguar, he said what in this day and age would have been standard procedure, the evidence that could have lead to the the real killer of Angus Sibbet lay inside of that green Mark X Jaguar, modern day DNA techniques could have found out exactly who the blood in the car belonged to, what is certain is that it was not that of the victim, or the two men convicted of his murder. I recently saw pictures and an interview with Michael in a local newspaper, lying on a hospital bed with tubes coming from his nose and mouth, ventilators helping him to breath; he is suffering from ill health with a heart condition. Is he asking too much to be heard by an appeal committee? Has he not the right to see his conviction quashed now, rather than have it happen after he has thrown off his mortal coil?

While incarcerated he achieved degrees from the Open University, although he was refused the option to study law. He is also a very accomplished painter and has a very impressive portfolio of work.

Two appeals were earlier rejected after the judge stated that he didn't feel there was enough new evidence to change the minds of twelve jurors. How can anybody be so arrogant as to assume to know how 'twelve good men and true' would interpret the new evidence from the forty or more witnesses who came forward with statements that wholly contradicted the prosecution's case? There was only forty five minutes when the two men could not provably account for their whereabouts, these were the forty five minutes that the prosecution had to bend, twist, stretch and concoct their case to fit into that small time frame. Yet even with all of the information now available it was decided that a third attempt at an appeal would not be granted, the judge decided that there was 'no reasonable chance of success'. To my mind it defies comprehension.

If the case was heard today, and that letter was to fall on my doormat asking me to attend court for the purpose of jury service, I would expect to hear *all* of the available evidence, and *all* of the available statements. Bearing in mind I would be dealing with the lives and futures of two people standing in that dock, I would feel I owed it to them and to society to hear every word from every single witness, no matter how trivial the prosecution believed them to be. Faced with what I have discovered while researching for this book, I can only imagine myself sitting in the court juror's gallery. I am being asked to consider, 'beyond reasonable doubt' the case before me. Beyond reasonable doubt, three words that mean in the eyes of the law, *'that no other logical explanation can be derived from the facts except that the defendant committed the crime, thereby overcoming the presumption that a person is innocent until proven guilty.'* I would retire with my fellow jurors to consider the verdicts to be passed onto these two men. I cannot find it in myself to agree that Angus Sibbet died at the time given by the prosecution; the only time that the two accused men could possibly have been responsible. It has raised a 'reasonable doubt' in my mind. I also need to express my cynicism towards the Judge and prosecution in how they seem to write off decent good people as being morons who must be making mistakes in their testimonies about seeing the Mark X two hours after the alleged murder yet saw no damage to the car nor a body inside it. In my imaginary court scene I hear the Judge asking the foreman of the jury to stand to announce his verdict. I can only hear two words echoing around that courtroom, '*Not Guilty!*'

"Science has proof without any certainty. Creationists have certainty without any proof." (Ashley Montague)

The End

N.B. In June 2011, Vincent Landa died from a pulmonary embolism, he was seventy eight years old. He was found at his Essex flat, he had lay there for three weeks before being discovered. Michael did not attend his funeral and was quoted in the press as saying, "I am not a hypocrite and would not attend the funeral of someone I did not respect".

Acknowledgements

Most Unnatural: An inquiry into the Stafford Case by David Lewis & Peter Hughman

http://villain-or-victim.com

http://innocent.org.uk/cases/staffordluvaglio/luvaglio_stafford.pdf

Mad Frank by Frankie Fraser

Nipper by Leonard Nipper Read

Journal/Evening Chronicle NE Media

BBC Archives

Britain's Gangland by James Morton

The people of South Hetton

5.15am from the album Shangri-la by Mark Knopfler

Innocent man fron the album An Innocent Man by Billy Joel

And finally to my Dad, for his patience and endless support, for which I am eternally grateful.

To everybody including those who wished to remain nameless, whose help was invaluable during my research for this book.

If after reading this book, you believe that there could have been a major miscarriage of justice and would like to show your support, please take the time to sign Michael Luvaglio's online petition, every single signature counts:

http://www.petitiononline.co.uk/petition/miscarriage-of-justice-united-kingdom-luvaglio/3483

For information, updates and news about the author:

http://stevenlytton.blogspot.com

Also by Steven Lytton:

'It's Because I Love You'

&

'Smoke Without Fire'

Printed in Great Britain
by Amazon.co.uk, Ltd.,
Marston Gate.